Praise for *Ready, Fire, Aim*

"Melissa Carbone is passionate, funny, and really smart—but most of all, inspiring. This book will give you the confidence to get to the next level in your career and your life."

—Michael Rapino, CEO of Live Nation

"Melissa Carbone has wowed people with her talent and guts. *Ready, Fire, Aim* is bold, actionable, and a rare opportunity for aspiring entrepreneurs to get personal mentorship from someone who has really walked the path."

—Jason Blum, CEO of Blumhouse Productions

"*Ready, Fire, Aim* is a refreshingly candid and real approach to making bold choices, relentlessly activating and fearlessly daring to capture the dream life. Its approach is accessible to everyone and incredibly inspiring. This book will become a bible to the next generation of entrepreneurs."

—Jillian Michaels, *New York Times* bestselling author, leading fitness expert, and life coach

"Melissa Carbone really breaks down success into an actionable process that is both inspirational and vulnerable. In *Ready, Fire, Aim* she allows her personal stories to be shared as examples of her topics and makes the content so impactful. This book is a beautiful example of entrepreneurial inspiration."

—Marty Singer, entertainment power attorney

READY, FIRE, AIM

READY, FIRE, AIM

How I Turned a Hobby Into an Empire

Melissa Carbone

BenBella Books, Inc.
Dallas, TX

BenBella

BenBella Books, Inc.
10440 N. Central Expressway, Suite 800
Dallas, TX 75231
www.benbellabooks.com
Send feedback to feedback@benbellabooks.com

Printed in the United States of America
10 9 8 7 6 5 4 3 2 1

Library of Congress Cataloging-in-Publication Data is available on request.
ISBN 9781944648961
eISBN 9781946885050

Copyediting by Scott Calamar
Proofreading by Greg Teague and Cape Cod Compositors, Inc.
Text design by Aaron Edmiston
Text composition by PerfecType, Nashville, TN
Cover design by Emily Weigel
Jacket design by Sarah Avinger
Cover photography by Chelsea Lauren
Printed by Lake Book Manufacturing

Distributed by Perseus Distribution
www.perseusdistribution.com

To place orders through Perseus Distribution:
Tel: (800) 343-4499
Fax: (800) 351-5073
E-mail: orderentry@perseusbooks.com

Special discounts for bulk sales (minimum of 25 copies) are available.
Please contact Aida Herrera at aida@benbellabooks.com.

This book is dedicated to my mom, Cathy Derench,
for being the example of a strong woman
that every kid should be lucky enough to have,
and for your relentless belief in me.

CONTENTS

INTRODUCTION

It was a perfect Los Angeles night in early June when the crunch-time pace of the Ten Thirty One Team started to escalate. The amount of banter I heard over the walkie-talkies was getting so excessive that the crew's frustration of not being able to get their sentences out was also escalating. A line of almost a thousand people stood waiting, with sleeping bags under their arms and packed coolers by their feet. As I walked toward the gates to open up camp, I jumped up on the back of a golf cart to gaze out at what looked like a massive crowd of people who had come to spend twelve hours of what we promised to be sheer terror. This was our most extreme attraction. An attraction that promised a level of interaction that would leave campers vulnerable to being bagged, caged, tied up, and more.

Who would want that? Plenty of people.

"Welcome to the very first Great Horror Campout, campers," I exuberantly announced through the megaphone. Screams and cheers, as if this crowd of people had just won the lottery, came right back at me. "Camp is open."

As the gates were unlocked the campers funneled their way inside and checked in to their assigned tents, setting up their home away from home for the long, dark night ahead of them. From there, it was a waiting game until it became completely dark. Nothing would start until then. Finally, over the camp loudspeaker came: "Well, howdy do, Camp Creepers. This is your friendly camp headmaster requesting the honor of your presence at the base camp flagpole for mandatory camp orientation. That means right the fuck now."

As if the headmaster had a leash on their necks, the mob of campers happily obeyed and marched to base camp. The headmaster was salty, vile, and offensive, from the way he looked—sporting his perfectly tailored tuxedo and shined shoes with a skinned and charred face—to the F bombs and off-color jokes coming out of his mouth. He made it clear there was no room to not listen to him. "The first rule of camp is that I can change the rules at any time for any reason and without notice," he said, letting campers know he was in charge. And finally, thirty minutes after he started his insanely entertaining and colorful orientation, with a David Lee Roth high kick to the air, he cocked his head back and held the microphone over his mouth as he screamed, "The Hell Hunt starts NOWWWWWW!"

A legion of campers jumped to their feet and went running into the dark to start what was going to be the game that would leave a few lucky ones crowned Hellmasters in the morning. They would dive for ribs in cadaver bodies, clip fingers off live characters, get kidnapped in vans, find themselves caged, and everything else a reasonable person would be terrified of. But these people paid for it.

The empire was born.

The Ready, Fire, Aim philosophy is one that dictates immediate action. It means you must take that shot instead of thinking yourself into inaction. It means that you should take many shots before someone else even has their gun out of their holster. Once an idea has grabbed you and your belief, it's out in the world and, if you don't capture it, someone else will. This philosophy is about jumping and jumping first. It's not void of direction or aiming. It's about starting and aiming as you go . . . It's about guts.

I wanted to create these very immersive worlds around the horror genre because I wanted more of it and loved it and was already involved with it as my hobby. There was nothing like it in Los Angeles at the time, so I decided to start "firing." This book is a detailed view of my thought processes, lessons why they worked, and why you can do it too.

As an adult I've really started to recognize the impact my mother's choices regarding her own life have had on me.

As a kid I'd see her making bold move after bold move even when the choice would throw her into the abyss of uncertainty and discord. I'll get more specific later, but the deeper I go into my reflection of where the "Ready, Fire, Aim" in me actually started, the more acute the consciousness becomes that growing up watching that kind of tenacious bravery was a big part of the foundation.

That realization has come to me many times, but never more loudly than on the day I appeared on *Shark Tank* and secured the largest investment in the history of the show.

The LARGEST investment in the history of the show.

It is already an extraordinary experience to get on that show, and an even more extraordinary experience to secure an investment from one of the elite "sharks." But this was the largest investment ever given from the most elite, most influential, and most successful shark on the show. Why? Was I lucky?

No! I "chose" it.

Even in the confines of an extraordinary experience, you can choose to act "commonly." It is more usual for aspiring entrepreneurs to appear on *Shark Tank* and ask for 250K, 90K, or 175K in exchange for significant percentages of their business. It is the "common" behavior of entrepreneurs on the show. And this by no means minimizes the boldness of those entrepreneurs, as the choice to even appear on the show is a bold one. It's an intimidating and highly vulnerable place to position yourself, and one that scares many entrepreneurs away.

But my proposition is to be bold to the boldest end of the spectrum. Leave nothing on the field; leave nothing on the table. Don't be reasonable . . . don't be rational. What great invention or societal change ever came from being reasonable?

Shark Tank had reached out to me a year or so before I appeared on the show, and I declined the opportunity. Choice. I declined because I was not interested in selling equity in my company, Ten Thirty One Productions. We were growing on our own and I didn't think we needed it.

Ten Thirty One Productions is an entertainment company that creates, owns, and produces live productions in the horror space. We own the most popular Halloween attraction in the country, among other events and live entertainment brands.

A year or so later, the producers of the show again called me to appear. They wanted to do a Halloween episode and feature a company that could bring a more theatrical flair to the season. I recognized that being on the show would be an incredible promotional platform for my company as we were planning our expansion into other markets and could really use the spotlight that *Shark Tank* would cast on us.

I still didn't want to sell a piece of my company, but I agreed to go on the show if they were amenable to my investment price tag being much larger than any amount that had ever been asked for in the past. It was the only way I could go on the show. I didn't expect any of the sharks to take the deal based on the high investment I named, but I had to make sure that, on the slim chance somebody did, I could live with it.

So . . . two million dollars it was! And only for a 10 percent equity stake in the company.

I completely expected the reception to my two-million-dollar ask to be less than warm. I expected to be held to the fire; I expected to be laughed off the show. I didn't care. I was going to meet my moment, be bold, and choose a path that would take me only where I wanted to go.

And, as it so happens, Mark Cuban lives boldly too. After a bit of negotiation, he took the deal, and to my sincere shock, became my business partner that day, making us the biggest deal in the history of the show.

I didn't follow the usual behavior of other entrepreneurs on the show to navigate my choices. I chose to build my story the only way I wanted it to start. There is a whole second part to the *Shark Tank* experience that we'll talk about later in the book, which pertains to preparing yourself to be successful in that type of situation, and business in general. But the first part of your success story is going to be rooted in the choices you make, and it is critical that you don't look to the choices of the general population to navigate. Look to the innovators, the 0.1 percent, the rule makers. Don't aim to copy them, but choose to be as bold or, better yet, bolder.

Have the audacity to choose to be even more successful than the most successful person you see. Then, activate and activate hard.

You've made the decision to "choose" boldly and put yourself on your path. And it has to be a way of life, not a one-off or something that you compartmentalize. This is the marathon, the long road trip that will inevitably be a very intense, emotional, and scary route.

Think of it like a diet. When people go "on a diet," the inference is that they will go "off of it" at some point . . . and, thus, gain the weight back or go out of shape again. It is those who change their diet or lifestyle who stay healthy and fit. And again, if we look at these percentages, they follow the same curve. The vast majority of Americans are out of shape, overweight, or unhealthy. They are "common," and those who choose to take a more bold path and stay healthy and fit are sadly "uncommon," or the 10 percent.

You are making a commitment to create greatness at all cost.

What's next?

No choice can start to live, breathe, and become a tangible accomplishment without arguably the most important ingredient to a meaningful existence.

You must take action; you must *activate*.

I cannot stress this point enough other than to have named this book, "Activate," which was, candidly, what I wanted to call it.

A choice without activation is a dream that is never realized. An idea without activation is a thought that never comes to life. A life without activation is a hamster wheel.

Part I

BUILDING AN EMPIRE

1

CHOICE

I wanted to be a rock star. And I was sure I would make it. I was probably five. The older I got, the more confident I was that I was going to make it.

That's where it started . . . an unrelenting drive that stayed with me and grew as I grew. I know this lays up the question, "What happened to the rock-star goal?" I'll get to it. This book isn't about hitting the bull's-eye every time. It's about using every piece of the story to build an extraordinary ride of success, love, risk, and confidence.

At this moment, I'm the CEO of a very hot company that is the first of its kind. We are poised to be the leader of a multibillion-dollar industry simply because I jumped into a pool that wasn't really on anyone's radar as a viable business due to the perceived "seasonal" nature of it.

My partners include one of the most influential billionaires in the world, the most powerful entertainment company in the world, a genius hippie who I call the Mayor of Burning Man, a couple of friends who invested in the fetus stages of the concept, and my ex-wife, who I was with for almost ten years. That's quite a melting pot . . . and the perfect storm.

I've experienced great success, great love, great loss, taken enormous risk, rebelled from societal norms, been exiled from family, made a lot of people love me, made a lot of people hate me, and I wouldn't have it any other way.

The path to get here started the moment I would not entertain any other life course than Rock Star.

The power of choice exhilarated me. I chose not to listen to the rationale of probability being spit at me by my father, teachers, schoolmates, etc. After all, I lived in a small farm town in Connecticut where rock-star level successes weren't common. And that's where my divergent path started. I didn't understand why being "common" was supposed to be the chosen path. After all, we're talking about choice . . . to do anything in the world. *Anything.* So, why common?

The concept of making bold choices is what starts extraordinary stories, and it's the best way to begin your success.

Bold choices are scary by their sheer nature, and because of that the majority of the population opts for "common" and thus lives commonly. The smaller percentage of people who choose boldly will either fall harder or soar higher. I will never guarantee you that making bold choices will result in success every time, but I will guarantee you that it's the only option to living your very best life. And if your choices are rooted in passion, belief, and follow-through, even setbacks or failures will inevitably sling you forward as long as you learn and keep going.

I never said it was easy.

Most people desire financial independence and judge "success" based on that metric. But the harsh truth is that the top 10 percent represents 86 percent of the wealth in America. The top 0.1 percent represents 46 percent of the wealth in America. Whether you think that's fair or not, that is an extremely small number of people holding the prize. It would be more "common" to be part of the 90 percent or the 99.9 percent not holding the prize. In this instance, it's easy to see why the societal push to do the "norm" or what's "common" doesn't appear attractive. However, I am going to propose that even in the not-so-obvious scenarios, the "choice" should most often (dare I say "always") be to fall in the 10 or 0.1 percent.

But unless you're the heir to a fortune, marrying somebody wealthy, or winning the lottery, it isn't going to be easy.

If it were easy, there would be more than this small percentage of the population enjoying this echelon of financial success.

It is not out of your control. You are not a victim of circumstance. You *are* your choices.

The fear of not making it, not being able to pay bills or afford to send kids to college, even losing social status among peers, keeps us handcuffed to being "common." But you are not handcuffed. You can jump at any time . . . you can choose to make a bold decision to start an extraordinary path.

I grew up on a farm in a very small town. But before that, my mom and I were on our own after she left my father when I was four. She had nothing, not a roof over our heads, no heat in our car . . . no money. She did have a job.

We moved around weekly to different family members' houses while she picked up tutoring jobs. She spoke fluent French and figured out how to make extra money using that skill. She could have easily stayed with my father to avoid the financial hardship that leaving caused, but she made the harder choice to leave and choose freedom. Not financial freedom in this case, but another kind of freedom. I watched her struggle and make the harder choices because her quality of life was her priority. Eventually, she fell in love again, and we all moved to a small run-down farm that my mom and soon-to-be stepfather purchased against the advice of everyone around them. Not one person supported their purchase of this farm. It was swampy, haunted;

it smelled terrible . . . everything that makes you choose to walk away.

They saw something much different, and even though this property was more than they could afford, they jumped. They spent the next five years working nights and weekends cleaning up the property by hand. As it started looking better and better, those who had warned against the purchase of the farm began to slowly eat their words.

It became the most magical place on earth.

To this day, it's a sanctuary to people and animals from all over the country and the most beautiful space you could ever imagine. My mother and stepfather have homed senior cows, horses, goats, donkeys, geese, ducks, dogs, feral cats, rabbits, and more for thirty years. The local community visits on "open house" days to interact with the animals and have the visceral experience of farm life. The local high school and college even support internship programs for students who volunteer to work on the farm with the animals. My mom and stepfather have saved the lives of thousands of beings and instilled a program that teaches compassion to the community. My mother has literally become a hometown hero.

Her choices impacted me enormously.

She chose to leave my father when I was only four. She chose to struggle. She chose to work every moment she was awake. She chose more struggle and more work so she could own a run-down property that her family was telling her was a ludicrous move.

She was the definition of "making bold decisions." And she created the life of her dreams.

So what happened to my dreams of being a rock star?

The answer is probably going to really surprise you.

I went after it, hard. And I started young. My mother got me a guitar when she saw it wasn't just a phase. I quickly started taking guitar lessons, and off I went with my instrument, making friends with other kids who were also interested in music. By the time I was fifteen, I started my first band called "MuSKAteer" during the time ska bands like No Doubt and Sublime were becoming popular. It was difficult to find players, but I did it and, within two months, I had written an entire set's worth of songs and booked our first show in Willimantic, Connecticut.

The crowd seemed to like us. But as with many bands, we had personality conflicts and quickly broke up.

My favorite band in the local music scene was a naked punk band called "Sorry Excuse." And yes, I do mean "naked." It was a band of three men ages eighteen through twenty-two, and, lucky me, they were auditioning for a lead guitarist. I was a giant fan and incredibly nervous to audition because the thought of being a member of one of my favorite bands sent me over the moon.

Even at this young age, I went after it with everything I had. All the odds were against me as a sixteen-year-old girl who could barely play lead guitar. I learned every song on their albums, forward and backward, and wrote a lead guitar part to all of them before my audition. On a super-cold winter day in Connecticut, I went to my audition in a barn with no heat, freezing hands, and played my ass off.

I got the part. I was now part of the naked punk band, Sorry Excuse.

I went on to play my first show with the band at Barrington College in Vermont. The very last song of the night, called "Touch Butts," was our cue to show the audience what punk rock was all about, the moment the packed crowd had been waiting for all night . . . the moment we were to get naked.

And we did.

Although, being a sixteen-year-old girl, I got less naked than the boys. Still, while my mother knew I was in the band, she had no idea nudity was involved. After the show, photos started circulating, my mother caught a glimpse of them, and that ended my naked punk-band days. After all, I was still living under her roof. Though I did try to be punk rock, and tell her where she could go with "her roof," it didn't really go my way.

I now had two bands under my belt and felt really confident that the third one would be the charm. I was seventeen and had just started dating a girl. My mom was thrilled, as she didn't have to worry about the things that come along with daughters dating boys. And the girl I was dating happened to be a virtuoso drummer from Berklee College of

Music with a virtuoso brother who played the saxophone. This was the start of what became known as "Rudie Brass," an incredible ska band that grew very popular on the East Coast and began playing shows opening for bands including Creed, Blink 182, Mighty Mighty Bosstones, and Goldfinger. I was the manager, guitarist, and vocalist of the band, and I managed this group like a business, booking shows almost every weekend, meeting with record labels, and doing anything it took to move us forward.

We stayed together for four years and did really well, but I was nearing the end of my college career and thinking about what was next for me. I had started to become disenchanted with playing music for a living. The members of Rudie Brass also started fighting, and personalities and a divergence of our ultimate goals began to interfere with us going any further. I've always said that passion is paramount in any success story, and my passion for this band started to wane, and with that, so did everyone else's.

My relationship with my girlfriend became rocky and we fell out of love and broke up. It was my first heartbreak and damn did it hurt.

So, I was going to jump.

I had never left the East Coast and insatiably wanted to experience big business and be close to the action of iconic success stories. I was hypnotized by tales of moguls like Bill Gates,

Warren Buffett, Oprah Winfrey, and icons like Clive Davis, Walt Disney, and so many others. People building empires were now the most interesting people on earth to me.

I rejected the internship program of my university because I didn't see anything that looked exciting to me. Even then, I needed passion in my life. I was able to get my university to accept a new program that I was going to create. I was going to find an internship that exhilarated me and put me exactly where I wanted to be . . . in big business with icons.

I worked for months trying to get in touch with everyone on the list above, and others too. I didn't care where or how long it took me, I was going to get my dream internship. This was my opportunity to get my foot in the door. And why would I want my foot in the door anywhere that didn't lead me to my dreams?

And I did it. I got an internship at Arista Records in Beverly Hills, California, working as a junior publicist. *I was going to be working for Clive Davis*. It felt like the greatest day of my life.

It wasn't a paid internship either but I didn't care. I would have paid them for the opportunity, if I'd had the money. I don't even think paid internships existed back then.

Once I finally regained consciousness and got off the floor, I remembered I had never even left the East Coast. I didn't know a single person in Los Angeles. Where was I going to live? How would I pay rent? Where would I earn money to eat and pay for life? All these thoughts lasted for thirty seconds, then I thought: *Who cares? I'm going into the great unknown and I'm going to be a huge success.*

The first day I ever set foot in California was the day I moved there. And because of that, I was very unfamiliar with the area and neighborhoods, and ended up living in an unsafe, high-crime part of town that was known for its gang activity and police corruption. I didn't have a car so I used public transportation exclusively. I had no money—I needed to work as much as possible when I wasn't at Arista Records so I put in applications at over sixty businesses. It felt like it was taking too long for any of them to turn into interviews, and I started really getting scared. I'd call home crying because I wasn't eating. My mom would put whatever she could afford into my bank account, but she couldn't keep doing that. I'd make peanut butter and jelly sandwiches and buy twelve-packs of Coca-Cola, and that's how I survived. Did I mention I was terrified? My supervisor at Arista could see that I wasn't eating very often and, on internship days, she would buy me lunch, which was like hitting the lottery for me. Finally, after a ton of follow-up calls, all those applications started hitting at the same time, and I didn't want to decline any job opportunities to make real money, so I took three jobs in addition to working at Arista.

I'd work at the Coffee Bean and Tea Leaf on Larchmont starting at 5:30 AM until 2 PM. I'd then grab a bus and go all the way across town to get to my 4 PM shift at Virgin

Megastore, which used to be on Sunset Blvd. I'd work there until midnight, at which point I'd walk six blocks down the road and pick up shifts as a cocktail waitress at The Body Shop, a local strip club. The Body Shop paid the best so I wasn't giving that up. I'd leave by 3 AM, get home and sleep for about forty-five minutes, and get back up and do it all over again. This lasted about three months until I landed in the hospital with exhaustion.

I made the choice to jump into an incredibly intimidating world that I had never seen because I believed this was the road to my bold goal. I thought so far outside of the "common" space that my college didn't even have a protocol for what I wanted to do. So I created it myself.

This decision took me off the Rock Star path and put me on the Building an Empire path. I was twenty years old.

And today as I sit here writing and reflecting on all of it . . .

I have an empire.

Coming off my internship in Los Angeles, I had managed to overcome my previous intimidation about working in large corporate environments with incredibly smart and influential people. The internship also gave me a pretty relentless work ethic and the ability to approach almost anyone, which pushed me to get back to Connecticut, graduate from college, and hit the ground running to start my career. It was like an itch I couldn't scratch. I was ready. I loved the thrill of achieving and was so inspired by the possibilities. I picked out what I thought was the coolest job in Connecticut, which wasn't really a hub for the entertainment industry. I found Clear Channel Entertainment and that's where I wanted it to begin. It wasn't easy to land that job, but after three months of interviewing and taking assessments and keeping myself at the forefront of their minds by calling and sending notes very regularly, I kind of gave them no choice but to offer me the job. It was the beginning of my born-and-bred corporate American career that would be so influential in teaching me the skill set that I needed a decade later to start Ten Thirty One Productions and live a life of personal freedom and happiness.

The ability to be bold and live extraordinarily started the second you began to make choices for yourself. Have your choices put you on the path to your best life? If your answer is "yes," congratulations. You are part of the 10 percent. If your answer is "no," I have really good news for you . . .

Your choices start now.

2

ACTIVATE

Operate, switch on, turn on, start, set going, trigger, set in motion, initiate, actuate, energize . . . ACTIVATE.

Everyone on the planet has ideas. Sorry to disappoint you, but you're not special because you have an idea. You're not even special if you have an epic idea.

You must activate on your idea, activate quickly, and activate relentlessly. That is the only way your idea will make you special. Often, even a mediocre idea will make you stand out when you bring it to life, because your sheer audacity to activate your idea right from the start makes you uncommon.

This is the decision maker. This is where the millionaires and billionaires are made. This is where leaders are born and where societal change happens. This is where life becomes extraordinary. This is the good stuff.

In this chapter, we'll focus on taking action toward career success on extraordinary levels. This won't come through doing just enough to get by or putting in a normal work day. Your best ride, owning your own time, means having a gladiator's work ethic.

People view success differently, but the constant is that it comes only through taking action—activating. And we don't just turn these traits on in a bubble; remember, it's a way of life. Being a relentless activator will help all the corners of your life, because even in personal relationships and beyond, committing to persevering through hard times and failures or sticking to your vision through thick and thin will ultimately uncover the answers.

I challenge you to think of one instance in your life where you felt proud or accomplished and didn't activate to get yourself there.

I own and created Ten Thirty One Productions, which single-handedly put Halloween and haunted attractions on the map as a viable business. It was a dark-horse industry that was raking in billions of dollars yet was not being developed the way other billion-dollar industries were being developed.

The day I quit my comfy, fat-cat, golden-handcuffed, lucrative corporate job at Clear Channel Entertainment and Media to develop a Halloween haunted hayride, the president of the company looked at me like I had three heads.

In fact, the whole Los Angeles–based staff that I had known for ten years almost to the day thought I must be certifiably, downright nuts. Their knee-jerk reaction lasted for about eleven seconds until they remembered who I was—the girl they had known me to be for so long.

I was the girl right out of college who interviewed relentlessly for almost five months, competing with seasoned veterans for a job I barely understood.

What I did understand was that in Connecticut, the best company in entertainment was Clear Channel, a media conglomerate dominating the broadcast radio industry, so . . . that was where I needed to land. I was the girl who got the job and peaked a year and a half into that job. And I was the girl who wanted to be in a market where I could grow faster. That's how I got to Los Angeles. But it wasn't as easy as it may sound. There was really no reason for the president of the Hartford Clear Channel market to give me the job. I was green and right out of college, but damn did I want it.

After a quick eighteen months working for Clear Channel in Hartford, which was considered a medium-sized market, I got to a point where my income started to plateau signaling I may be at the point of maximizing as much growth out of that area as I thought would be possible. I have always been motivated by forward and upward movement, so I knew that if I didn't activate soon, my passion in my work would suffer, and that has never served me well. I need to love what I do. I learned that the Los Angeles market was a large one and the *largest* revenue market of all the markets . . . #1.

I decided to start there.

I picked up the phone and called every Clear Channel Los Angeles radio station and scheduled interviews for the four out of eight that responded to me. It took a ton of follow-up to get them to meet with me, but once I finally secured the four interviews, I bought my ticket for the cross-country trek to LA.

Though I was interviewing for the same company for which I was currently working, I chose to keep it quiet. I didn't want to alarm my current managers just yet. I knew I was valuable to them and my departure would not be a welcomed conversation. But, hey, I was staying with the company. I could have scheduled interviews with competing Los Angeles properties and I didn't, so my moral compass felt in order.

The trip resulted in a job offer. I was moving to Los Angeles to work for the biggest revenue market in the world.

What happened next floored me.

Upon telling my direct supervisor of my fantastic news, she fired me on the spot.

In fact, a colleague of mine, who also wanted to make the move but had not yet secured a job offer, was also fired on the spot for even entertaining the idea.

Nope. I wasn't going down this way.

These are the moments that define the "extraordinary path" or the "bold choice." I had never been fired in my life, and I wasn't about to let that change.

I tracked down the vice president of the market, Paula Messina, who to me was a reasonable and strong woman. There weren't many female executives ranking this high in the company at that time, so my hope was that she would be fair and strong enough to care about the injustice.

And I was correct. She was very appropriate to make sure she didn't throw any of her appointed managers under the bus. She told me to go home early and take a little time off while she worked through it with the manager who had fired me. I got a call two days later, telling me to come back to work.

And to make things even better, I was asked to stay for three months before taking the job in Los Angeles so they wouldn't be shorthanded with the extensive list of clients I had grown to manage and be responsible for. They offered me a large bonus if I were to accept. Upon the approval from my new boss in LA, I stayed for three months and signed off in Hartford as a valuable, loved, and missed part of the team.

This was a much different and far better path than having just accepted being fired. I activated. I didn't just take my serving of "shit pie" and go home.

In fact, remember the colleague I mentioned earlier who was also fired that day? She didn't activate; she didn't push the issue, and guess what? She never got asked back, did not leave the company on good terms, and spent the next year unemployed.

I chose this company and I activated to make it happen. I chose Los Angeles and I activated to make it happen. I chose to leave the Hartford market on my terms and I activated to make it happen.

Your path is up to you. I experienced evidence of that, and in each instance like this, my faith in my choices and my belief in my abilities were growing.

I was twenty-three years old and on my way to LA to work for one of the biggest entertainment companies in the world. This would be the move, the choice, the activation that would bring me down the path to a soul-mate love that lasted almost a decade, the path that taught me how to run every facet of a business, the path that would bring financial wealth for the first time in my life, the path that exposed a confidence in myself that would lead to my unreasonable notion that I could do anything . . . live my very best dream life.

I was young and I was new. Many of the big, scary, tenured LA executives barely gave me a nod to welcome me. As I remember, only one girl, who was also new, invited me to lunch and asked me about myself.

Within my first year, I had developed more revenue and received more top performance accolades than anyone on my team. I had an amazing mentor, Michael Jackel, who was my boss, and I soaked up every bit of coaching he would give me. I watched his demeanor; I listened to his vocal inflections; I absorbed his interactions with other managers and important clients. While my tenured colleagues were lunching, I was watching.

This industry was sexy and exciting. Passing Ryan Seacrest in the halls coming in every day to work, Cher, Pink, the Black Eyed Peas stopping in to promote their albums or do private concerts in our offices—this was my workday. I understood how it could get distracting and how it could jade those who have been around it regularly. But this was the hardest industry in the world to get close to, and being around it wasn't cutting it. I wanted to lead it.

There were several managers in the company, but Jackel was a leader. There was a quality in him that I found infectious and I wanted it. Now, over a decade later, I can finally identify that quality as *passion*. It is so easy to become addicted to passion. It's a critical part of the curriculum and we're going to discuss it more in later chapters, but I'll start by saying that activating when you are passionate will never feel empty or feel like work. And this is a great barometer for you when you are on the fence about a choice. Passion will guide you honestly.

Jackel was, in his own right, moving up in the company, and if I had anything to say about it . . . so was I. By the time I was twenty-six, I took Jackel's spot as the local sales manager of the second-largest-grossing Clear Channel property in the country. He kept moving up and I kept moving up. A couple more promotions and, before I was thirty, I was controlling the revenue for multiple Clear Channel Los Angeles properties, which made me the youngest manager in the company controlling more revenue than any other single manager globally. For all practical purposes, I was running a business.

This wasn't luck. This was pure activation built on a foundation of hard work. I worked for my track record so I could make my own choices and go after them. I didn't wait for opportunity to knock. Every manager to whom I reported knew I wanted to be a leader. I *was* a leader whether I had the title yet or not.

You will give yourself a big head start by acting the role to which you are aspiring before you even have it. People will get used to you for that role and, when it's available, you'll appear as the natural progression or fit.

My time at Clear Channel was also the time in my life when I met my partner Alyson.

We met when I along with a couple of my colleagues were interviewing her to come work at Clear Channel. She was very impressive, and it was easy to decide that we wanted her on the team. As the interview ended, I remember my boss turning to me and saying, "The two of you have a connection; she likes you, take the lead on this and get her on board."

I'm pretty sure I loved her the day I met her. We became inseparable. I'd get nervous to see her and excited to go to work. There were times when I'd be thinking about her and she'd appear next to me.

I remember running down the beach in Santa Monica one day by the pier. I had my headphones on, probably jamming out looking like a fool, and I felt someone running right beside me. I turned my head and there she was. She had seen me from off in the distance and had run her ass off to catch up. It was a karmic feeling right from the beginning. I knew she would be a big part of the journey.

My ascension into management was also about the time I started to earn the reputation of "Ready, Fire, Aim," and that was fine with me. That was a giant compliment, in fact. In an existence where being an activator is how you achieve dreams and the unthinkable, that was the ultimate compliment.

Remember, it means that I'll take a hundred shots before my competitor's gun is even out of their holster. And I may miss half of them . . . but that means I hit half of them too.

The scariest part of activating is the fear of missing.

I've seen many talented and hard-working people who aim so diligently that they aim or think themselves into inaction. It's a bit cliché but the simplicity of the quote "the only shots you're guaranteed to miss are the ones that you never take" is the essence of its effectiveness.

I know "it's not that easy." Guess what? It really is that easy! Take the shots. You're going to miss sometimes but what is the alternative? Mediocrity at best? That's probably okay for many people, but I'm guessing that if you picked up this book and are still reading, that it isn't good enough for you. It certainly isn't good enough for me.

The dirty little secret here is that once you miss, the fear of missing starts to fade. Once you experience a failure and bring yourself back from it, the fear of failure starts to become less paralyzing. Walk into the fear and I promise you it will never dictate your path again. You must use your "miss" or your "fail" as a piece of data. Study it, break it down, and understand it. Then, take another swing with the new information. The fear of failure will no longer stop you from activating.

I have failed and failed big.

Ten Thirty One Productions—TTO—was founded in 2009 with one attraction called the Los Angeles Haunted Hayride. I was still employed by Clear Channel at the time, which is so incredible, thinking back on it now. I can't believe they allowed me to launch a giant Halloween attraction while they still employed me. I was even able to convince them to let me advertise it on our eight Clear Channel Los Angeles radio stations. And to add more shock and awe to the irony, the Clear Channel sales team was tasked with going out and selling sponsorships to my event. I think I must have under-estimated my sales skills.

By this time, I was becoming burnt-out with the corpo-rate environment and had felt like I had gone all the way up the ladder but wasn't learning what I needed to in order to stay engaged. I didn't feel like I was really growing anymore.

Halloween was rolling around, and every year I deco-rated my house to an obsessive degree. Each year, Alyson and I noticed more and more children coming through our yard display. We also noticed their parents mingling in our front yard and many of the kids going through the yard attraction more than once. We counted over three hundred children and it started to occur to me that Halloween just might be a big deal.

Could this make money?

Instantly, I started to research the industry, and it wasn't hard to find out that this was a six-billion-dollar business at that time. Now, it has grown to $8.4 billion.

For a market the size of Los Angeles, I was beyond shocked at how underserved it was for Halloween activities. I have loved Halloween my whole life, and spent my entire childhood going to haunted attractions and, more specifi-cally, haunted hayrides. I could not get enough of them. I would wait for hours to get on the local haunted hayride in town, and then scour the area to find other haunted hay-rides. I had always wished for a haunted hayride in Southern California but year after year . . . no luck.

A lightbulb appeared over my head as I discovered the revenue behind this holiday and the lack of girth it had in a city the size of Los Angeles.

I had wished for a haunted hayride every year, and now we would have one.

I didn't wait; I didn't think myself into inaction; I didn't let anyone talk me out of it.

I activated.

I woke up and created a list of all the parks with trails and woods in Los Angeles County, got in my car, and physically inspected all the sites. I was in permit negotiations two weeks later. I had no idea how I was going to pay for this as the ice-cold reality of expenses started to strike. However, I wasn't going to let someone else do this before me. Alyson and I went to a few of our very close friends and asked them to invest. None of them are independently wealthy people, but they believed in us. They believed we wouldn't lose. Some of them asked their parents for the money, some of them used every last penny of their savings, but somehow they each scraped up the money to buy 1 percent of our new business.

We approached many potential sponsors as another revenue source. It's really hard to sell a sponsorship for an event that has no track record and no large corporation behind it adding validity. We just kept pounding the pavement and finally secured an auto sponsorship from MINI Cooper for $75,000. Using what we had in our savings account, combined with the sponsorship funds and the small investments from our friends, that very next October, LA got its first-ever haunted hayride.

The Los Angeles Haunted Hayride has become a Hollywood Halloween icon.

This doesn't sound like a failure because we haven't gotten there yet.

Activating my idea brought this company and LA Haunted Hayride to fruition. It has been the biggest game changer of my life. My dream life was upon me.

The Hayride didn't make any money in its first year, and there were many giant obstacles with permits and political bureaucracy standing in our way at every turn. But even with the uncertainty of whether the LA Haunted Hayride would grow into a viable business, I took a giant leap.

I resigned from Clear Channel after a decade. It was the only company I had ever known. The company where I was born and bred a corporate protégé and felt safe, secure, and comfortable was now in my rearview mirror. It was a hard decision for anyone in my life to understand except for me and Alyson.

Being comfortable wasn't a good thing, and I didn't need anyone else to understand. I had chosen my path and now I'm walking down it . . . not halfway down . . . all the way down.

3

DISNEY OR BUST

I n March of 2009, as I walked into the largest industry trade show for Halloween attractions, I didn't know a single person except for a farmer from Pennsylvania who was teaching me the intricacies of building a haunted hayride. And I loved him and still do.

One of the first things I did when I decided I was going to build a haunted hayride was to research the others that existed around the country. There were none in California, so I studied hayrides in upstate New York, Connecticut, Oregon, Maine, and Pennsylvania. The one that overwhelmingly seemed to get most of the accolades was called "Bates Motel and Haunted Hayride." I happened to catch it on a Travel Channel special and was very impressed by the owner of the attraction. He had a glow and warmth about him but also seemed like a businessman, as well as a farmer. He appeared to have the whole package. I tracked him down that day and left him a message.

He called me back less than an hour later. Clearly, he was an activator too. I was elated to hear on the other end of the phone: "Hi, Melissa. This is Randy from Bates returning your call."

I think we spoke for a good hour that day. I asked him some very proprietary questions, and he never hesitated to give me the info. I asked him how many people he hosted in a season, average ticket prices, ride length, hay wagon dimensions, who he used for vendors. He gave me all the details. He even invited me to come to Pennsylvania to get an inside look at his goliath attraction. I couldn't believe how amazing he was. And needless to say, after that phone call, I was off to the races.

He told me about an industry trade show where he'd be speaking that year and asked me to attend. I was ecstatic to find there was a place I could go to learn everything I needed to know about my new industry. It was the Disneyland of Halloween. I had visions of revolutionary meetings with the brains behind the best that Halloween had to offer. I'd strike deals with inventors of scare technology who would be only too thrilled to work with me on my brilliant new Los Angeles attraction. Vendors would be waiting in line to schmooze me all weekend long in the hopes of garnering my business to add to their portfolio. After all, I was building a brand-new, world-class Halloween attraction in the sexiest city in America. I could see the red carpet being rolled out as my plane landed in St. Louis.

But to my surprise, the trumpets quickly turned to sounds of deflation and blooper bells. After arriving at my hotel, I walked through the lobby to check in to my room. There were what felt like hundreds of people littering the lobby of this three-star (at best) hotel. The chatter and sound of voices was loud, and the bar was buzzing. I remember seeing a lot of black T-shirts, sweatshirts, and jackets with logos. As I looked closer, I noticed the logos featured names of haunted attractions.

Holy Moly! There were hundreds of different Halloween attractions being represented in one room in March. Halloween in March sounded great to me.

Once my overwhelming excitement stabilized, I also started to notice that the vast majority of this crowd was male. Actually, it was all male. That night I didn't see one other woman adding to the buzz of that hotel lobby.

I thought it was odd but wasn't uncomfortable about it at all. I was sure there would be more female-owned attractions represented on the show floor in the morning.

I bounded out of bed and my hotel room the next morning ready for the start of my empire.

As I walked into the giant, sprawling expo hall for the first time, it was like arriving in Oz. Fog billowed out of the doors; before the entryway was even in sight, the latest and greatest in creatures and characters were slinking their way into my personal space. Sound effects and strobe lighting were bleeding out of the hall. This was just incredible.

As I finally made it inside the hall, I saw Randy from Bates, who had now become a mentor of sorts. He started introducing me to his friends and colleagues. Some were vendors, some were attraction owners . . . all were men. That first year, I met only one other female attraction owner. Only one. I would like to add that her attraction was probably one of the best in the country . . . but still, only one. I was flabbergasted. She had a giant attraction in the Midwest that I had heard was incredible. And instantly, I could tell she didn't like me. Her demeanor struck me as cold, which puzzled me since I thought she'd be elated to see another woman in her space. Looking back now, I've deduced that this population of independent haunt owners was just incredibly competitive. That must have been what I sensed that day.

As I started moving deeper into the hall, I began to notice that I was pretty interesting to the people in that room. My male counterparts seemed to be addressing me with what felt like a bit of a condescending, "What are you trying to build, little girl?" As I was explaining my vision, I felt dismissed. Los Angeles was like a different planet, and my audacity to be a little girl in a big man's world seemed to offend them or somehow demean the industry that they felt was all theirs.

I understand that I am overgeneralizing here, but that was how I was feeling. I met several very nice and helpful individuals, but the vast majority of what I was encountering felt very intimidating.

My mentor, Randy, is like the Halloween attraction OG, so luckily I was rolling with the best and able to get a giant education in a short weekend from all the introductions he was making for me.

That weekend I decided I would produce the most professional and publicly visible attraction in the country, if not the world. I'd come back the following year and mean something different in that space. I had no problem proving myself, and that is exactly what I was going to do. Not just to these dudes in a room, but to myself. I'd never walk into this convention feeling intimidated again. That was my promise to myself.

I have a ton of respect for the owners who have run a successful attraction for ten or twenty years or more. It's hard to keep any business successful for that amount of time. But I was interested in making this a living, breathing, evolving company that always had something new on the horizon. I didn't want to wear a black T-shirt with a haunted hayride logo on it for the next twenty years at the trade show. I wanted my logo, symbol, and name to be a ticker symbol on Wall Street. I wanted to see my company logo in every major city in America and beyond. I saw a huge opportunity in this industry. It seemed to be a giant industry of thousands of independent owner-operators. And these days, that's become rarer in any viable industry. I felt like this space was mine for the taking.

"Let's start small."

Those words make me feel ill. I would rather gut myself with a fork then ever hear those words in business again.

For starters, we should put the word "small" in context. I'm not here to suggest that you shouldn't jump or activate on something if you can't bust out of the gates as a billion-dollar funded venture. But I am here to suggest that you have to throw every goddamn thing you have in your veins at it. It should never feel like you're starting small. If you're putting every bit of your sweat equity, hustling, and spending your own resources to make an idea live and breathe, I promise you, you'll never describe it as small.

"Starting small" feels like the plight of the reasonable. Do you think being reasonable is going to get you into the 0.1 percent? I'll tell you that the answer is a certain no.

We live in a world where there is a place for "small," medium, large, extra large, just like there is a place for poor, wealthy, obscenely wealthy, happy, depressed, Ivy League, uneducated, lawmakers, criminals . . . you get the picture. Where will you place yourself? If you want to be small or mediocre at best, then start small. I'm not your girl, and chances are I'm just going to piss you off if I haven't already.

But it's easier for me to watch a movie like *Martyrs* or *The Green Inferno*—where people are being dismembered and eyeballs are being squished between teeth like maraschino cherries—than it is to watch a person with the guts to take a shot, and the tenacity to activate, "start small" and not leave every part of their constitution on the field.

It is very important that you do not mistake what I am saying, as my message is first and foremost to activate. For crying out loud, let's become a nation of activators. However, this is now about giving you the best shot for enormous success once you do activate.

If you want to open a local wine bar that super serves a five-mile radius, with an intimate and moody setting and a capacity of forty people, that's fantastic. I'm not telling you that it should be ten times the size, franchised into two hundred cities, and traded on Wall Street. I'm saying to put everything you have into making that wine bar special, and owning your space in the marketplace. Be the best and only wine bar anyone will think of when on your side of town. You certainly wouldn't want to open your doors to the public with less than a perfectly polished aesthetic or without introducing yourself with your brightest impression. What if I said: start small, don't waste money on marketing, or don't paint the outside as long as the inside is painted. Let's keep the staffing light, let people find street parking, and we can get new furniture and start featuring better wines once the money starts rolling in.

Now, on the other hand, imagine instead that opening day is approaching and your wine bar has been teased in all the food-beverage social media and local blog sites; a local radio host has chatted about it during his morning show; the morning news is broadcasting live on opening day; you've even put your new, sexy logo on a few choice billboards in your target area. Menus are freshly printed; the bar décor is sleek, clean, and new; only the best wines will ever be seen in your bar; and your wine bar sign busts out loud and prominent onto the street for all who pass by to see. While inside, there is a full and well-trained staff dressed nicely, and a buzz has already started because a week earlier you did an exclusive sneak peak for tastemakers, media, and influencers. A friendly valet service waits at your curb to take the cars of your customers to make their experience as easy and inviting as possible.

This is the same business, but one started small.

Present yourself like you're Disney, right from the start . . . and the world will believe you. Present yourself like you are from Podunksville, and they'll believe you too. It is your theater of the mind, your image, your positioning to create. Don't mess it up before your customers even get to your door.

Coming from a marketing and advertising background, I knew this was where we could win or lose. I also knew how expensive it was to place marketing campaigns in Los Angeles.

Alyson and I had a small savings account, but nothing that could fund the creation of a major attraction with major marketing behind it. Regardless, we knew we would drain it to build this company, though it wasn't nearly enough.

The day after Halloween in 2008, I started my research and began looking for potential sites to host a haunted hayride. It was very difficult to find woods in Los Angeles, so our options were a bit limited. Candidly, those controlling the few options also knew we were limited and they could basically have their way with us. Making matters worse, I was wearing my passion and excitement for my new haunted hayride on my sleeve, so I was a neon sign that said: "Gouge me for every dollar I have." And boy, did they ever. While we found our dream location (at the time) very quickly, we had to negotiate with the mountain conservancy in charge of the land for almost six months, just to be told that there was a whole other permit process we needed to satisfy. And then we were late since that process can often take six to nine months. The woman in charge of granting the permit was almost finding entertainment or joy in holding the power to squash our dreams. I had to step aside from the conversations at some point to let Alyson take the wheel because I was literally going to slip a Mickey in this woman's environment-killing plastic water bottle, watch the drugs take effect, and then release the video online of her swinging from the chandeliers of a skanky motel . . . if skanky motels even have chandeliers. But in my visions of revenge, they did.

The plastic bottle is important because this woman worked for an environmental conservation group and always had a plastic bottle in her hand. My blood was boiling.

As we got later into the year, they had more and more control because it was now virtually impossible for us to open the attraction anywhere else. And at this time, we were unknown. The Los Angeles Haunted Hayride was just a weird-sounding farming ritual. We had very little influence. This is when I realized I needed a powerful lawyer who could bulldog his or her way into land-usage negotiations. But this was going to be expensive. We had already heard that just the location permit was going to wipe out our entire savings account, so we needed to really get focused on raising the money to make this dream real. After we paid for the permit, we didn't have any money to build anything *on* the location.

Alyson and I had good reputations among our peers, and I think it's safe to say many people around us felt like we weren't going to let ourselves lose. That's the first piece for me. I was living my life in a way that made people believe in my work ethic and tenacity . . . not just when I needed something, but long before I needed something. This is why I assert so often throughout this book that the desire to get on your bold and best path isn't something you can compartmentalize, it's something that has to be a commitment to every corner of life at all times. You have to grow it, want it, and commit to it.

Alyson and I created a very visually stunning presentation using video from the Randy Bates hayride and a ton of research that showed how incredibly viable and untapped the Halloween attraction market was in Los Angeles and nationally. We wanted to raise an additional $350,000, so our next step was approaching potential investors. And they weren't the typical investors that you might think we'd approach. We hit up our best friends and their parents first. These aren't "trust-fund baby" friends. These are friends who probably had less than we had. They didn't have an extra $25,000 lying around to buy 1 percent of a start-up that was all about Halloween and haunted hayrides. But to my utter disbelief, my best friend, Alyson's best friend, a mutual friend with whom we worked, and a client were the first four to jump on board. A couple of them had to get money from their parents, but they were so confident in us, and wanted to ride whatever wave we were riding, that they somehow did it. And percent by percent, we started getting back into the positives. We were still far from our goal, but we also decided we'd bring our presentation to some potential sponsors to see if we could make up the difference.

We created a list of things we could give a sponsor that included event real estate, inclusion in media, special discounts and incentives, and much more. And we both agreed it had to be a sexy sponsor. No Podunk Mama's Pizza from down the street . . . no way. We wanted something like BMW, Coca-Cola, Verizon, Best Buy. We knew with a sponsor like that, we'd have some instant street cred. Getting major brands like those when we had no track record and were a complete unknown would be a miracle . . . or take a lot of pounding the pavement. And that—pounding the pavement—I could do. Everyone can do that. I can't control miracles but I can control the hustle. In year one, I remember it taking somewhere to the tune of over a hundred phone calls to even get someone to meet with me. I was exhausted and so was Alyson. But now, it wasn't just our money on the roulette table, it was the money of our best friends and people who said: "We believe in you." That was even more important than our own money. There was no way I was going to fail the people who believed in us. And that kept pushing us forward.

The positive piece that came out of all the meetings, phone calls, and networking through our jobs was that we kept getting connected to other people so our network was growing quickly. And a client of ours connected us to a regional person with MINI Cooper and gave us an incredible testimonial, and guess what? You know it. MINI became our first-ever Los Angeles Haunted Hayride sponsor, and what a perfect sponsor they were. Alyson and I were elated. To this day, it still shocks me, and I still get choked up because I can't believe we pulled that off.

The program was incredible. MINI would offer tickets to the Hayride when potential customers test-drove a MINI, and on one coordinated event, MINI would rally a huge group of MINIs to the Hayride where we'd host them for a VIP experience. The sight of a hundred MINIs pulling into our parking lot that night was gorgeous. As corny as it sounds, I thought to myself, "If you build it, they will come," as I saw the line of cars waiting to get into the lot.

I started to tear up. I just couldn't believe we had done it.

Even with the MINI sponsorship, we didn't make it to our goal of $350,000, but we made it to $225,000, and with my and Alyson's contribution of our savings account, we decided we'd make it happen and figure out a way to creatively get whatever we needed but didn't have enough money to buy. I knew we would not sacrifice quality or our positioning in the marketplace. We'd figure it out.

We were going to burst onto the scene like we were Disney right from the start, and that was not negotiable. And our new, prestigious sponsor was the first step. We decided to use that money to place giant billboards all over Los Angeles. Talk about looking like you came to win. We hand selected every single billboard we wanted in LA so that every location was prime. We could only afford a small amount so they had to be beyond incredible. Location was the first consideration, and the artwork was the second. The art was captivating, enormously haunting, and colored like nothing else on the streets, which pulled people's attention to the boards right away. Within just a couple of days, we started getting flooded with emails and calls to our hotline with interest. We knew the boards were working.

The feedback coming from all our friends, our sponsor, and the general public on our hotlines was that our billboards were everywhere. If you lived in Los Angeles, you could not escape the Los Angeles Haunted Hayride.

Then, our radio advertising went live. And yes, I worked for Clear Channel but I still had to pay for the campaign. I got a discount for ten years of service to the company, but it was still a chunk that was hard to swallow. Every dollar that we were spending on advertising had to come from the set construction or staffing or casting. But I was determined to figure it out.

We did the same thing with our radio campaign as we had with our billboards. We cherry-picked the best times of the day, best stations, and best content with which to align our campaign, and again, the buzz was loud as hell. I heard every single day, over and over, that the LA Haunted Hayride was everywhere. People would tell us that it must be nice to have endless buckets of money to build a new business, and probe us to find out how much money it took to launch the haunted hayride. Little did they know how creative we were getting behind the scenes.

While the marketing and advertising campaign was set in place early so we could focus on operational activity, as October got closer, we hit a pretty giant snag. The production partner who had come on board to build the sets, produce all the sound, lighting, and special effects decided a month before we were to take possession of the location that unless I paid him $100,000 up front, he couldn't do the job.

My head exploded. We didn't have the cash to pay him. The deal was that we'd pay him upon completion of the event with our ticket revenue. And the fact that he waited that long to tell me that one very important bit of information brought me to a conclusion that he was probably not the best fit; he would not be a partner I could have faith and confidence in for many years to come. I called his bluff and told him that I was terribly sorry, but that just wasn't going to happen, and we would be there to pick up our equipment and end the partnership immediately. I wasn't that polite about it. This was long before I learned the very fine art of powerful communication in the interest of not igniting a world war. Even though sometimes in business going to war is warranted.

Alyson and I were at it again, hustling our asses off to find a solution. Our best friend knew of a guy who was a creative, brilliant mind. While his business acumen left a bit to be desired, he made up for it with his inventive visions. And candidly, I didn't need a business partner at this point; I needed someone who could build a beautiful Halloween world that Alyson and I had created earlier that year. I needed someone who could pick up the ball, see the vision quickly, and execute it. But again, I needed to get imaginative because I didn't want to wind up in the same position with our new production partner, so I offered a percentage of our ticket proceeds for that year in exchange for his services. It appeared our passion and belief in the project was infectious, and he agreed. We were back in action with less than a month until our install was to begin. And with our new production partner agreeing to a revenue-share deal, I could keep our cast and staffing at the ideal levels. No quality compromise or reduced performance would occur in any department.

Marketing and advertising were firing on all cylinders. The town was buzzing. Influencers and high-profile personalities started coming out almost every night; our new production partner was even better than the last; the cast, wardrobe, special effects were gorgeous; and cars were lined up to get in. Year one, and this town thinks they're at Disneyland.

I couldn't ever start small. Excitement for "what could be" was too high, and the fun I was having as I learned about this new industry, which I was loving more every day, was growing rapidly. With that kind of emotional investment, the anguish and anxiety are overwhelming. I can't tell you how many times I called my mother, hysterical, telling her I wanted to pull the plug, and that this level of stress just wasn't worth the health issues and disease I was sure it would bring me later in life. But you are somehow able to get through those low moments when your belief in what you are doing is so strong. And though we are leaps and bounds bigger now than we were that first year, we were huge that first year. It's still my favorite year and the one of which I am proudest.

I often say that bringing the LA Haunted Hayride to fruition that year was a miracle, and doing it on our own terms, calling the shots like we were Jay Z and Beyoncé, was divine intervention. That divine intervention is called faith . . . in your own ability to move mountains, faith that you have every tool you need to get anywhere you want to go. Yes, you can even build Disney. And I did and do believe that every day. I don't think there is anything I can't do, and that is a gift and a confidence that came with taking enough shots to know that I can get there eventually.

The next important piece is to deliver your positioning. Present yourself like you're Disney and that will get them to your door, but once they are there, you must make sure they have an experience that matches. You need them to come back in order to create a sustainable and growing brand. The way you introduce yourself to the world should be the beautifully polished red skin of the most perfect apple on the tree. That will get your audience to reach up and pick you, but what will they taste when they bite into that gorgeous apple? Will they spit out that first bite or take another and then another?

You must deliver an experience that aligns with the image you create. You introduce yourself like Disney, you provide a larger-than-life experience in every way, and the world belongs to you.

The best way to be consistently extraordinary in your offering is to stay very involved in your creations. Even when you are successful and growing rapidly, find the path that keeps you involved. Often that is finding incredible talents walking the world that share your vision, passion, or have the eagerness to learn it all. Create more leaders who can help you divide and conquer, and still stay involved in all of it. You can grow slowly. Grow at a pace that is conducive to birthing only extraordinary content. When you learn that the world is connecting to what you have, opportunity starts to roll, and to roll quickly. It's hard to turn down opportunities because it can feel like you're turning down growth or money or prestige. But taking an opportunity that isn't right can cost you the time and power that would have been better spent pursuing opportunities that are exponential to your growth, and it can also cost you quality of your already-existing assets. The balance of opportunity and growth is strategic. The first priority must be to never compromise the user experience and quality of your offering. If by taking on an opportunity, you become unable to keep your business, brand, and experience looking, feeling, and tasting as epic as it was when it was your only focus, then pass on the opportunity. The time will come for the growth to happen as long as you stay great.

Starting great and staying great is oversimplifying a bit, but I think an easy cerebral putt. Starting your own empire with the polish of the royal family, the attention to detail of a Michelin restaurant, a user experience as easy as a warm knife going through butter, a marketing voice as loud as a Midwestern thunderstorm, and a leader as hands-on as

Justin Timberlake during a wardrobe malfunction is going to show the world you mean business. And every bit of what it takes to do that is within your capabilities, and well within your reach. You have everything you need to do it. Get creative, get strategic, and, most importantly, get moving. Every move will provide a piece of information to push you to the next move.

The first move is yours.

4

FAILURE

Of course with every high comes a low. I can still remember the way my chest felt from the minute my eyes opened in the morning to the moment they closed at night . . . that is, if they closed at all.

I was constantly reassuring myself that certainly thirty-four years old was far too young to have a heart attack. But it didn't matter; it felt like my world was falling down around me. Thinking back, I am quite sure that this was also when my marriage started to suffer.

It's just business, right? Wrong. When you have wrapped all your money, your friends' money, energy, time, love, into taking a risk, there is no way not to be emotionally invested.

And it's incredibly idealistic to assume otherwise. But this, this was worse than I could have ever imagined.

I was actually getting death threats. The one thing I hadn't expected was that the launch of a new Halloween attraction would ever end in having to fear for my safety. It sounded ludicrous to me.

Ghost Ship was our second attraction and brand. And I must start by saying, the concept is incredible, and it's an attraction that I will bring back using the hard lessons and uppercuts to the jaw I took that year.

It was the definition of our company philosophy to create attractions that have never been created in their respective markets, and to create them in environments that have a built-in mood of being haunting, creepy, disturbing . . . before we even put our blueprint into the space. This was to be the first haunted attraction to take place on a ship that actually would set sail into the dark, open ocean at night. There are haunted attractions on ships but not ones that actually set sail. The dark, wide-open ocean is the most haunting part, so it seemed like an obvious move that had been missed. And I wasn't going to miss it.

I activated and began my search for a ship with the girth and capacity to house an entire attraction with hundreds of people.

To this day, I think Ghost Ship was beautiful. I had a hard time figuring out what went wrong when the first patrons started to complain. Were there opening-night kinks? Was I too close to it to see that it actually really sucked? This was our second attraction, and it was taking place in October 2011 simultaneously with our giant attraction, Los Angeles Haunted Hayride, which was already iconically popular. Two attractions happening at the same time meant I couldn't be at one of them every night. Had I taken on too much too soon?

We were, by that time, well-known in Southern California, so we even had a built-in population to whom we could market our new attraction. We publicized it as "From the Creators of the LA Haunted Hayride," and you could almost hear the swoon of Halloween fans far and wide twitching with excitement.

That was mistake number one.

Ghost Ship was built for the forty-something, disposable-income Orange County, California demographic. It was themed booze cruising, so to speak. The passionate Hayride fans wanted terror, blood, guts, and content that would epically ruin them for life.

The wealthy folk of "the OC," who rolled up in their Benzes wearing their Rolexes, ready to get hammered on the high seas, actually had fun and liked the ride.

The nineteen-year-old cult-horror lover, who had sixty bucks to spend to pick one attraction for the season, then figure out a way to get from LA to the OC without breaking the bank on gas money—just to arrive there and have to spend the night with a boatful of the aforementioned demographic and not even be old enough to drink—was pissed.

It may not sound like a big deal. Some liked it, some didn't. The problem was that the demographic that liked it wasn't the demographic that was all over social media and vocal about it.

The conclusion of each voyage added to a wave of negative Yelp reviews, Facebook comments, and threads on Ghost Ship press articles. At first I thought we could pull up from the nosedive by adding more content, making some changes in timing and capacity of the voyages, but nothing seemed to work. Nothing was effective because I was not yet aware of what was going wrong. People were getting angrier and angrier and now starting to feed off each other's anger. I couldn't believe how angry a Halloween attraction could make someone. A mob was growing.

I reached out to our publicity team at the time and asked for help. They saw the magnitude of the rumble and basically left me to deal with it on my own. They wanted nothing to do with what was becoming the redheaded stepchild of Ten Thirty One Productions. They wanted only to be associated with LA Haunted Hayride, which was getting rave reviews.

I decided to take to the Facebook page and start addressing the anger. Remember, this was my creation, my blood, and I was emotionally attached. When someone calls your baby ugly, you want to lash back. And naively, I did just that. I had noticed there was a group of aggressors, or haters as they were often referred to, who appeared to be friends and worked for another Halloween attraction in Orange County, so I quickly jumped to them as my scapegoat and called them out on social media.

By this time, I had already been losing sleep, having panic attacks about this attraction being the downfall of my company. This was *my* company. I had always had the insulation of a corporation behind me, so this kind of fear and anxiety was new territory.

I chose to attack back, and that was a really bad move. The Ghost Ship bashing quickly turned to Melissa Carbone bashing. There is no doubt that I can be hotheaded, and it really clouded my judgment in that moment. I basically started a mosh pit on social media. It was me against them. Join me or die. I took to the social waves ready to go to war with every bad commentator I could find. I'd prove them all wrong and, at the end of the battle, stand victoriously on top of the mountain of slayed bodies of my social media enemies. I'd say things like "Your misguided hostility is polluting these pages," then ban them from the page, or call them bad seeds. In direct emails with people, I'd have full-blown arguments. These were my customers and many of them were Hayride fans. The snowball was getting bigger, insults growing more vicious, the social media attacks started moving onto the Hayride social platforms, which I knew I had to stop. The Hayride was our flagship and if that was too adversely affected, it could be a fatal hit.

My final breaking point was the online posting: "Does anyone know where Melissa Carbone lives?" *What?* It had gone too far down that road, and it was obvious this had gotten way out of hand.

The nucleus of the problem originated from the fact that we had built the attraction for one demographic but marketed it to another. The passionate Hayride fans were the ones buying the tickets. After all, everywhere you saw the illustrious Ghost Ship logo, the tagline "From the Creators of the LA Haunted Hayride" would follow. And instead of tackling that as our issue, I created a much bigger one by declaring war on everyone who dared to judge our blood, sweat, and tears.

And now someone wanted to assassinate me! Yup, that's what being an asshole gets you.

That was the turning point or the day I started learning how to become a much better problem solver and communicator.

Alyson was feeling the brunt of my mania and I remember we were fighting a lot. I was ruining the thing in the world that mattered most to me, which may be surprising, but it was not my career—it was my life with her.

Alyson is very safe with her decisions and I'm very risky with mine, so the two of us together were a match that worked very serendipitously. We were both exasperated and concerned. Her cautiousness really came in handy at that time. She stopped me in my tracks and made me really look at what I was creating. I needed to get out of my own way and figure out how to de-escalate the angry mob, not pour lighter fluid on their already flaming heads.

We started to implement big changes on Ghost Ship to make it more extreme, and invited people to come back again (on the house) to try it out. If they didn't want to do that, we invited them to be VIP guests at the LA Haunted Hayride, where we treated them like royalty. I individually spoke with each and every angry customer in a tone of offerings and solutions.

The tide starting changing, and I took note of how learning effective communication was one of the most important things you could do for your company, relationships, career, and every other multiperson endeavor that crosses your path.

Our customers wanted to feel heard and know that they had value. I realized that not everything would be successful right out of the gate, and to be an effective leader and entrepreneur, I would have to learn how to really hear the problem to fix, reinvent, or rebuild it.

Ghost Ship didn't pull up from the dive, but we stopped the bleeding, which was the best alternative at the time. We stopped it late in the game, though, because I unfortunately didn't start communicating effectively until the last week of the attraction.

It took a little while for me to bounce back from that one, personally. I can't tell you how different it feels to have a corporate leviathan behind you. When I worked at Clear Channel, I was the same hotheaded, mouthy executive that I was when responding to my Ghost Ship haters. However, at Clear Channel, I knew it wasn't my money, the money of all my closest friends, and ultimately my life being threatened or celebrated. If I lost money, missed budgets, or produced a failing event, other than the shame I'd feel internally, it really was someone else's money lost or problem to solve. That's a much easier environment to harbor self-righteousness.

But the other side of that is when you win, hit budgets, make tons of money, and produce epic events, it's also someone else for whom you are making the money and whose empire you're building. And that wasn't a choice I thought would lead me down my most extraordinary path.

I believed in myself and it really was just that simple. Don't misunderstand for one minute: the education I got from growing up as a corporate executive was invaluable. But now, I was willing to fail in order to learn the things I could never learn under the wings of a corporate entertainment giant.

It would have been easy and safe, in the short term, to make it to the end of the season never to revisit Ghost Ship or any other new ideas again. We could have just stayed with our sure thing, LA Haunted Hayride, and had a cushy, mediocre success story. But remember, we have the choice to do anything . . . to be extraordinary . . . to take our best ride.

So let's get up, wipe the blood off our chins, get some veneers to replace a couple lost teeth . . . yes, take some time for a breather to get our focus back and strategize using the pain of the past and then, hit it even harder.

Only world domination will do.

5

PERSONAL STRUGGLE

The *Hollywood Reporter* came out saying: "Sneak Peak! The Biggest Deal in *Shark Tank* History Could Happen This Week."

Right away, calls started coming in from my friends, family, and associates who had seen the article.

"Oh my God, Melissa, did you get the biggest deal? What happened? This is so exciting. Can't wait to see the show."

There was a flood of excitement from the people in my life. I didn't say a word. I couldn't. I waited until the show aired. And on October 25, 2013, it did, and that was it—the biggest deal in the history of the show had happened. I got the deal and Mark Cuban, world-famous billionaire, was now my partner.

It was a fairy tale, an entrepreneurial fairy tale.

And it was all real. The shock on my face was real. I truly had no idea it was going to turn out that way.

What nobody saw were the moments before I walked into the tank and the few minutes before that. And with the exception of my therapist, best friend, and mother, these pages are the first time I have detailed it publicly. And even now, I take a deep sigh as I bring my mind back there to tell the story. The critical status of the wounds have subsided, but the scars remain and I am still very careful in my mental hike back to that time.

On that morning in late September, when the show was being taped, I was on the studio lot early to get prepped to film our pitch to the panel of sharks. My creative directors, assistant, and some cast had come with me for the pitch, as we had a scare in store for the sharks. I felt like I had on a pretty good game face. It took everything I had. The buzz about our pitch was very high, and I could see the producers and crew were really excited about it, so I don't think anyone could tell I was in any kind of emotional fog.

This was the opportunity of a lifetime. We were to be the first pitch into the tank, and that was amazing news for me. A beautiful and elaborate set was put in place for our pitch, complete with gore and horrifying characters. The crew was incredibly nice and helpful with every part of this process. As it got closer, I did notice their excitement increasing. And candidly, I was getting nervous.

Remember, not one person knew how this would turn out, if the outcome of our presentation would be successful or not.

The sharks had no idea I would be standing in front of them in a matter of minutes with a legion of monsters trying to make them pee themselves.

I had gone into a pretty elaborate process of hair and makeup, and now had been politely placed in a green room by myself to wait to be called into the tank.

It was the first moment of silence I'd had that day. As everything around me stopped, I could no longer try to ignore that I was dying. After an almost decade-long relationship, Alyson and I had split about four months prior, and I wasn't making it. To try to explain the dire straits I was in would be futile, as I don't think it can be conveyed at all. All I can say is that, truly, I was dying. I was critically suicidal, had started drinking way too much, and was taking prescription drugs. She was my entire world and she was gone.

Sitting in the green room, the realization that I was there without Alyson knocked the wind out of me. Starting what could be the next chapter in Ten Thirty One's evolution, taking it to a national audience of millions and potentially making the biggest deal we'd ever made, felt empty. Intellectually, I knew that I needed to take the time to really feel this moment because it would be over quickly. But I couldn't feel anything except sadness. I couldn't go home and celebrate with her or cry on her shoulder if it turned out badly. I couldn't call her; I couldn't see her; I wouldn't have her ever again.

I lasted about three minutes in the green room before the unrelenting pain of missing her crept back to find me. It never let me get more than a few minutes away from it. As it gave me my usual kick in the stomach, I got dizzy and started to have a hard time breathing. I sat on the floor welling up with tears, as my perfect makeup job poured down my face. I kept telling myself to get my shit together, but I started to worry that I couldn't pull myself out of this in time, so, as if things couldn't get worse, I think I started to have a panic attack. All of this from the girl who used to get overly yet quietly annoyed when someone cried in the workplace. I hated that and didn't feel like there was any room for it in a business environment.

A quiet knock, and a voice came through the door alerting me that we'd be going to the holding room outside the tank in a few short minutes. I got up off the floor and started to wipe my eyes. I was so embarrassed. I had to get up and meet my moment. I don't think it's overdramatizing to say that I wasn't in my right mind, but I know that my passion for business and the opportunity that I had in front of me was one I would regret blowing if I were to survive this breakup. And even if I didn't survive it, this wasn't going to be my mic drop.

The production assistant came back to let me know it was time for us to head to the *Shark Tank* doors. Maybe I'm being oversensitive, but I think he looked at me, like, "oh shit," and I'm pretty sure it's true because the makeup person miraculously showed up to fix my face. As the countdown clock hit sixty seconds before the doors were to open and I was to start the walk down that long hallway, the makeup artist frantically brushed here and patted there and, with a second to finish, the doors opened, cameras were rolling, and to the tank I went.

While I was very good at applying my lessons to the professional sector of my life, sadly I was still neglecting the nosedive of the most important relationship I had ever had. I mentioned earlier how communicating effectively can have an enormous impact on essentially every multiperson experience in your life, including relationships and love. Unfortunately, I learned that more quickly in my career than in my personal life. While I was getting a handle on the Ghost Ship nightmare, my relationship with Alyson was being tried daily.

I understand the fear of failing intimately. I was terrified of failing in all aspects of life. Not just my career. I was even more terrified of not having meaning or purpose. I felt like a star when I had been at Clear Channel . . . I knew I was the best. I was confident and exhilarated by the fast-ladder climb of my tenure at Clear Channel. I had no idea how valueless I would feel the day after I resigned.

One day there is a line out your door of people who want you, need you, aspire to be you. The next day, when you don't have anything they need or want, it's incredible how quiet your phone gets.

I became my own worst enemy. I had jumped from a very high-paying job with importance to work by myself and "try" to build an empire. And that takes time. I was working every day at home alone, hustling to get people to take meetings with me. When you call from the world's biggest media company, people take your calls and meetings. Now, I was calling from an unknown new start-up that did not sound very sexy. Even contacts that I had worked with for years at Clear Channel were no longer available to meet with me.

It felt like shit.

What had I done? Talk about feeling like a giant failure, this epitomized my fear of failure. The thing I feared the most was coming true. Nobody cared about me. I was not important anymore.

The first problem was that I internalized my self-worth based on my career status and income. But that's a reality in our society. We are born, bred, and socialized to align our meaning in this world with our income and job title. It's not okay, but it's real and a hard demon to slay.

Alyson would come home from work and I would swear to God she was judging me because I was no longer a powerful corporate executive. My mind was spiraling. She was incredibly diligent about reassuring me, but it didn't matter because my mind was a storm of chaos. I needed to reassure myself.

She took on the responsibility for the majority of our living expenses so that I could focus on building our new company, and that made me feel like a freeloader. I couldn't get a handle on my insecurity, could not find my self-worth, and could not believe that the love of my life actually loved me just as much without my fancy, powerful, corporate job.

I failed.

Not at building the company, but in my marriage to Alyson and our decade-long soul-mate love. It took a long time but I really do believe that the initial stress of feeling worthless, and the different but subsequent stress as the company grew and became very successful, started to dent the armor of the relationship.

Our relationship failed for several reasons, but this was, in my opinion, the first crack of something I mistakenly thought was unbreakable. Most of those who knew us would have bet their life savings on us being together forever. Alyson's best friend once laughed at the notion of the relationship ever ending. I never saw it coming . . . neither did Alyson.

One night in San Francisco a couple years earlier, Alyson and I were having dinner with two of our close friends, Jess and Russ. We, or I should say, they, were having a really intense conversation about loss. As adults, Alyson, Jess, and Russ had all lost a parent, and it shook all of them to their core, as you would expect. They were talking about the coping mechanisms and the ability to keep memories close at hand. It was a pretty long discussion. I was silent through most of it. At one point, Alyson looked at me and gave me a little smile as if she could tell what I was thinking. And she could, because later that night, while we were alone, she said to me that she sometimes worried about me because she knew how close I am to my mother, and I've really had no loss in my life to help prepare me for that kind of life event. Sitting at the table that night, I was the only one out of the four who hadn't experienced death. I feel incredibly blessed for that, but it did provoke a nagging feeling inside that I could really get hit hard one day.

And ironically that day came—the day Alyson and I split up.

This wasn't a normal or average breakup.

I talk about living boldly as a way of life, not something you can activate when needed and then put in a sock drawer when you don't. So it makes sense that this breakup would be of epic proportions, because the love was of epic proportions.

We started having problems and didn't address them effectively or in time. I was mad at her; she was mad at me. I started to push her away until one day she didn't come back. I took for granted that she'd always be there. I gambled and lost.

Ten Thirty One Productions had a brand-new attraction on deck: the Great Horror Campout. It was slated to launch June 7, 2013, a month after our split. To say I was leveled doesn't do justice to my feelings at the time. It's hard for me to write about this time because much of it has escaped me. There was an almost ten-day period when I didn't get off my floor. I had a giant dog bed in my bedroom at the foot of my bed where I spent the better part of those ten days. I had dropped twenty-two pounds in about two weeks, was drinking two bottles of tequila a day, and wishing for death. My mother was a wreck and had also lost weight because of the situation. I hated seeing what this was doing to her but I couldn't stop it.

I started going to therapy almost every day. Sometimes for two-hour sessions. After almost a decade together, our lives had merged so I didn't really have any of my own friends. The friends we did have were in shock that our marriage was over and kept saying "you guys will get back together" or they'd say nothing at all because it was all so weird. I'd hear stories of Alyson showing up with her new interest, and it would send me back to my floor on that dog bed, so I soon decided I had to make new friends that were not connected to my old life. But it took me a long time to get there.

As the launch of Great Horror Campout was approaching, I knew I wasn't okay. Nothing mattered to me without Alyson. I created the concept; I pulled the trigger on making it our next attempt at a new attraction since the Ghost Ship chronicles concluded; it was my responsibility as the CEO of this company to ensure its success; but I was in hell. Honest to God, I was in hell.

I know I was physically present during the Great Horror Campout because I've seen pictures, but I can't recall any of it. I have an absolutely incredible team and leaned on my creative directors at the time, Justin Meyer and Melissa Meyer, to take the wheel. They did, and it became our second new brand, attracting a giant cult following. It was the brand that Mark Cuban was really interested in expanding. We've now done twenty Campouts in eight different cities. I hope that, one day, as the trauma of these past four years gets further away from me, some of these memories will come back.

6

REFLECTION

This was the first time in my life I was experiencing a loss that took me out. I'm sure the fact that I hadn't experienced a significant loss was a part of the reason it became so abnormally acute. I was supposed to be a machine. Nothing could stop me . . . until something did. The spiral kept going for almost three years and kept getting worse. I started riding a motorcycle, subconsciously probably hoping I would die. I would think about ending my life twenty-four times a day, but I was so worried about how my mother would cope. I had just seen her go through the death of her best friend, and it was awful. She couldn't come to terms with it. What would she go through if her only kid, whom she lived for, took her own life. I was also worried about my three dogs at home whom Alyson and I adopted together, two when they were babies and one when she was super old. What if nobody found them for days, and what if they went to a shelter until someone could come and get them? I couldn't stand those thoughts. Somehow, accidentally killing myself on a motorcycle felt more tolerable for those who loved me.

On October 7, 2013, I crashed my motorcycle.

I ended up in the hospital, with screws and pins in my hand and arm, a scarred left leg and knee, and three reconstruction surgeries later, I have about 80 percent use of my left hand.

And because I really wanted to see what I was made of, this happened in early October, which means I had to get through the entire Halloween season with the LA Haunted Hayride, a major attraction open for eighteen nights. This accident happened a couple weeks after the filming of *Shark Tank*. When that episode aired a couple of Friday nights later, I was at the LA Haunted Hayride watching our email blow up, unable to move my left arm, walk on my left leg, and trying to manage the pain of the injuries while I ran a thirty-acre attraction serving sixty thousand people at the time.

I was numb.

I had grown up with happiness everywhere around me. I had a blessed life of an amazing mom, fun childhood, excellent education, early career success, soul-mate love, wealth. And now it was my turn to fall . . . to hit rock bottom. The girl who got way too excited when she took a bite of something that tasted delicious or got to binge watch her favorite shows on vacation in hotels—her spirit had broken.

I started to suffer from depression for the first time in my life at thirty-six years of age, and after a nearly fatal dose of alcohol and drugs almost took me out, I realized I needed to try to get myself on track. Nothing had killed me yet, so I figured it just wasn't my time.

Having the realization that I was not only okay with dying, but wanted it, really spooked me. I had such a hard time understanding how I had become this person. But the truth is, I'd needed to become this person. I'd needed something to blow me up to make me pay attention. I think everyone on the planet has to go through their own version of this, because nobody is perfect.

I can honestly say that this pain forced me into an absurd level of reflection that precipitated into a lot of work . . . personal work. Personal work means different things to different people, but for me it was about being cracked open and made to look at where my ego and abandonment issues were navigating me. It was the terrifying moment I saw my father in me, an oppressive, combative, and overly opinionated man to whom I wanted no similarity. We have the choice through enormous pain and discomfort to either wait it out and let "time ease the pain" or to dig into it. Walk into that pain and deconstruct it; understand it to make damn sure we don't repeat history.

Too many people—or shall we say the 90 percent—let time go by as their solution to healing rather than digging in. Typically, the result is another failed relationship, another lost job, another moment of settling for mediocrity or less.

The work is hard, but a lifetime unsatisfied is unbearable.

As I sit here six years after that first hard fall with Ghost Ship, yet again I am on the heels of what has been another very difficult launch of a new attraction.

However, during the six years in between, we've had the most exciting and exponential growth imaginable. Had the fear of another failure made us tentative, reluctant, or just downright stopped us, we'd have missed it all.

We'd have missed the launch of the Great Horror Campout in 2013 that instantly became a smash-hit cult sensation, which went on to expand into nine more cities in its second year and is now going into its fourth year with hundreds of copycats springing up all over the country. We would have missed our brand-new Great Horror Movie Night series that started in 2015, which too has become a giant hit. And we would have missed the expansion of our flagship attraction to the East Coast, New York Haunted Hayride, in October 2015.

It can definitely be argued that bringing the Hayride to the opposite side of the country in New York City was a failure. In some ways, it was worse than Ghost Ship because it lost a lot of money. But in many ways it was so much better, because none of the mistakes we made were the same ones made on Ghost Ship. I'm sure some of you think I'm being overly "Kool-Aid" drunk or elitist, like . . . is a whole new batch of mistakes really better?

Yes, I do think it is. If you're in the outfield and get hit in the face by a pop fly, you learn to put your glove in front of your face. If you don't, you keep getting your face split open until you leave the sport. So, thank God, we are living true to our philosophy of examining the data of our failures, making the adjustments, and trying again. It's working. We don't want to leave the sport. When you stop falling, you stop growing.

Sure, it would have been wonderful for the New York Haunted Hayride to have been a grand slam right out of the gates, but it wasn't, and I am not afraid to get up and try it again for a third year with our new information because the second year got better and it will continue to get better. We have seen that it works firsthand. We can expand upon the equity we have already built to create a successful attraction in New York City, or we can hang up a "closed" sign and go back to the West Coast. That is the only way New York Haunted Hayride fails. We only fail if we ensure defeat by packing it up and taking it home.

New lessons will certainly come from this one that we will take to other markets on the East Coast and beyond, which will get us closer and closer to launching hayrides flawlessly. The growth is by definition exponential when you learn to correct and begin to look at failing much differently.

The things that go wrong are almost always aspects that can be turned around. The New York Haunted Hayride's number-one hurdle was that we picked a bad location. The accessibility of it was deceiving because it looks very easy for customers to get there, but it's not, because most people in NYC don't drive. Additionally, the culture in NYC keeps people in their respective boroughs with very little compelling them to go anywhere if it's not just a subway ride away. The location needed to change. That's fixable. Another problem we experienced that first year was the weather: we were having terrible hurricane-like winds and rain that left us swimming through the hayride instead of riding behind a tractor. That wasn't fixable. However, we can build our structures to be bomber proof so the winds don't break them in half and cause us triage work each day just to keep chasing our tails, which was another problem we experienced. If we could learn and remedy 80 percent of the issues, it's probably worth another shot.

My opinion of myself today is so much better than it's ever been in my life. The personal progress I've made from being blown apart into a million pieces and having to figure out how to put them back together in a healthier way has helped all the categories of my life. I don't align my value in the world with my career clout or income anymore. And that has been a hard demon to exorcise. My friendships are stronger; my career feels better and is more prosperous; my romantic relationships are so much more communicative; and I'm just happy . . . and I have even fallen deeply in love again.

It's important to let go of guilt and regret. I don't have regrets because it is all part of my story. I am equipped with the tools that I didn't have a few years ago to ensure the decisions and actions of the future will take me where I want to go. The tools are expensive, but not having them is more expensive, and it has to be real. Personal growth is hard . . . to me, it's the hardest thing I've ever done, so it has to be encountered with belief and passion to really work.

There are those who read the books, go to therapy, meditate, reflect, and swear to God they have conquered the mountain but then show with their actions that not much has changed. There is no mountain . . . no finish line. It is a constant practice, and one that requires faith in the process and in your ability to bring your mind and vulnerability to a high degree of awareness or consciousness.

This is by all means the place your most extraordinary life lives. Give it the time and attention it needs, and I swear to you with every ounce of belief that fits into my five-foot-eight-inch, hundred-and-thirty-five-pound body that in return you will discover success, wealth, love, and the truest meaning of taking your best ride.

Alyson and I have since found a new place as best friends, and it seems like that's where we have probably belonged for some time. The love and respect that we have for each other has made us okay. We've both gained a person who we know will be here always, which is more valuable than what we were as a struggling couple just trying to stay together. The ego and fear were kicked and vulnerability embraced, which enabled our story to have no end and, on the contrary, continue on better than it was.

I often say that I look at my career as a giant real-life game of monopoly. How much of the board can I control? How big of an impact can I have in my world? Don't get me wrong, as Halloween attractions started to flood the Los Angeles market, I had a serious "oh shit" moment. It was just a moment, but a moment that pushed me to realize I had to build revolutionary blueprints for live entertainment. This realization is what brought me to the philosophy that would become our mission and formula for everything we created. It's a philosophy that requires all Ten Thirty One live attractions to be the first of their kind in their respective markets. It's a philosophy that requires all attractions to take place in an environment that is innately haunting in its demeanor before we even put our touches into the space. And it's a philosophy that keeps our attractions refreshed every single year, meaning no two years will ever be the same.

This very philosophy birthed the first-ever Haunted Hayrides in the biggest markets of this country, the first and only haunted attraction that takes place on a ship that does actually set sail into the dark, open ocean at night, the first and to date only twelve-hour overnight horror camping experience in the country, and the first outdoor interactive horror-movie-night series in Los Angeles.

To keep the content changing every year requires an intensive creative process that never ends. All of the above attractions have provoked copycat attempts, so we need to stay a mile ahead at all times—to find new technologies, skill sets, or new ways to use sound, light, movement, and more.

"Learn to evolve or cease to exist" repeats in my head every day.

I started to see the power of sound in patrons' reactions to our startling effects and its synergistic relevance to the feeling of largeness. At the LA Haunted Hayride, we had been repurposing a full-scale burnt-down church each year. It was a beautiful set, but we just weren't getting the bang out of it that a scene with such grandeur and beautiful aesthetic should elicit. So I started to play with the idea of choreographed group movement to soundscaping. The theme was called "The Congregation" the year we finally nailed down the activation of this massive burnt church that had been lackluster for three years. I can still remember the moment I saw the visual in my head. I was sitting with Alyson in our home office late at night and, as it came to me, I started spitting out the idea faster than I could develop it in my head, which was often what would happen when something fabulous entered my consciousness. I had a vision of forty red-robed demons being subjugated by a horned devil priest who was also regally robed—set to sound in the most targeted way. Each movement by the twenty-five-foot rising priest and his red-robed, glowing-eyed congregation would be in unison to a bump in the soundtrack, until the final, grand sound cue would unleash the congregation onto the patrons as the glowing-eyed demons chanted in chorus while clicking sticks to commandeer the wagon, leaving the hay riders with a satanic chant that they just couldn't get out of their heads. This is complete immersion into our world.

To compete with the rising number of attractions coming into LA and the rest of the country, this immersive style of dropping our guests into a world was becoming more and more important. The spectator-sport type of live attractions was becoming the dinosaur. The one thing we do that I think is so unique and critical to our formula of staying ahead and reinventing ourselves each year is to bodily transport our guests into a world. Even theme parks around the country that go to a Halloween theme for the season will send you into gorgeously produced mazes and shows, but when you come out and have to walk five or ten minutes just to get to the next maze or Halloween attraction, you pass cartoons and giant themed rides that have nothing to do with Halloween: pastel-colored Dippin' Dots carts or SpongeBob popsicles. You are taken out of the world while you walk to the next environment. It's impossible to really submerge your audience into your narrative that way.

In all of our attractions, from the moment your car enters our permitted area, you are in our world. You can see the orange glow of the haunted hayrides leaking out of the tree-tops from the freeways. You can smell the hay in the air or watch the parade of campers with coolers and sleeping bags under their arms walking to check in at the Great Horror Campout. And we never ever take you out of that experience until you are in your car driving home. And even then, we often leave our guests with parting gifts of disturbia.

As we're talking about finding new ways to keep evolving in your space, it's important to find inspiration literally every-where. In 2014, one of our creative directors had been doing our usual endless amounts of research and development, and stumbled upon an acrobatic skill called "sway poling" that was being used in Australia and other countries, but not in the United States, and certainly not in live horror attractions. It was such a creepy and odd-looking type of movement. The problem was that there were no such skilled acrobats in the United States because we didn't sway pole here. And that was exactly why we needed them. We imported the troupe from Australia to spend several weeks in our warehouse to train a domestic group of acrobats in the skill of sway poles. We choreographed a world-class soundscaped sway pole vignette that blew the minds of everyone who attended the LA Haunted Hayride. In fact, once the Hayride wrapped, the sway pole buzz lasted and even got bigger. And low and behold, as the brand-new *Mad Max* movie was released over a year later, there they were . . . a major spectacle in one of the biggest action films of the year, if not decade. I was so proud that we showed the world sway poles before anyone else. And not necessarily because we did it first, but because it reinforces that we are doing great work. It reminds me that we are walking our talk, evolving and revolutionizing our space and the entertainment space more broadly. And yeah, I do love that we did it first!

Creating my company was like having a child. It's that level of commitment to create something for which you have enormous expectations. Why do it any other way? I want Ten Thirty One to win. I want Ten Thirty One to stand for something that the world recognizes as the leader, the visionary of a space that's really important to people. I don't want to produce spectator sports.

I will bring you into a world. And you may only be with me for two or three hours or even less. But I will push your head underwater into an experience that will deliver a narrative that does not stop until you have long left my reach. I will attack every sensory component that your brain can register through touch points, through spatial or strategic engagement, and through simple God-awful heart-attack-inducing fear. While you're with me, you won't be thinking about the shitty day at work you just had or the dreaded early morning workout the next day. The only thing on your mind will be wondering what the hell is coming around that next corner to ruin you.

Part II

KEY LESSONS

7

PASSION

f I asked you if you'd rather someone's opinion of you be that they think you're "okay, fine, not bad" or that they "hate" you, what would you choose?

Passion, by sheer definition, is any powerful or compelling enthusiasm or feeling like love or hate: a strong desire. The antonym or opposite of passion is apathy.

So the choices posed above are between the person feeling passionately about you or apathetically about you. Does that change your response to the question?

Of course, there are some qualifiers here to consider that we'll get to, but in theory, I'd say to love me or hate me is a very good indication that I'm living my life with passion. I know it's not a harmonious feeling to be hated, and this is not a play to convince you to start your day bounding out of bed with goals of collecting hatred toward you. But it is a play to consider that apathy is often worse, and that being hated isn't necessarily bad.

Being passionately loved or hated is often an indication that you are living with meaning, sincerity, or more simply stated . . . giving a shit. On the other side, being hated can also mean you are a murderer, tyrant, domestic abuser, or something evil to which of course none of us aspire. However, even in those excessively evil instances, you cannot deny the existence of passion. Tragedies of disgruntled workers committing murder in their workplaces portray them as passionately angry; Hitler passionately hated Jews; O.J. Simpson was passionately jealous; and all of these manifested into horrible occurrences, but occurrences that are nonetheless forever marked in history.

The positive footprints of passion around the world are obviously easy to identify, such as the end of slavery; the recent legalization of same-sex marriages; and more broadly, technology, music, art, activism, and more.

What's harder or even impossible to find is when apathy has been recorded in the history books. Where is apathy remembered?

"Passion" is a buzzword being thrown around often these days. "Follow Your Passion," adorns decorative frames, mugs, book covers in gift shops and retail outlets all over the world. I think I've even seen it as a tattoo on a person's body.

And it's most often used in the career sense: as if passion matters most when it can be monetized.

There are even business experts asserting their resistance to the "following your passion" wisdom, which has probably become so popular that it's begging to be debunked. A business expert on a panel discussion about passion recently threw Steve Jobs's name into it to validate his own assertion that following passion is overrated.

He stated it was evident Steve Jobs was on this bandwagon because of this reported response by Jobs to a question about the "Follow Your Passion" mantra:

> *Yeah, we're always talking about following your passion, but we're all part of the flow of history . . . you've got to put something back into the flow of history that's going to help your community, help other people . . . so that twenty, thirty, forty years from now . . . people will say, this person didn't just have a passion, he cared about making something that other people could benefit from.*

I don't see how this doesn't epitomize passion.

If you are looking at that quote for Jobs's passion to be about technology and computers, then yes, you will miss it. His passion was for giving the world something great, helping the world to progress and benefit on a large scale. His passion for that gave us the most accessible form of technology arguably ever created. Do you think if he were apathetic about making the world better or helping people he would have given us Apple? I may be wrong, but I don't see Jobs going into the office and throwing his coat on a chair and saying, I guess I'll try to revolutionize the world today and if I succeed, cool. He was relentless and unyielding in this desire, in his level of giving a shit, in his powerful and compelling feeling. This is passion's definition.

Additionally, in Jobs's comment, nowhere did he even assert that passion wasn't vital. He simply stated: "this person didn't *just have* a passion." It's more logical to interpret his statement to mean that augmenting passion with other ingredients is the lethal formula that bakes extraordinary.

Passion is not linear. In this case, his passion for helping people and moving the world wasn't about career. It collided with his career because that's how he activated to manifest what he was passionate about. But this is why we can't regard passion in such an obvious way or put it into categories like professional passion and personal passion—they aren't mutually exclusive, and there are literally no rules governing how we activate passion. Often people can't even identify what they are passionate about. They may discover they are really good at something and that fuels a desire; they may become educated about a topic that connects with them and compels them; or they may even be afflicted by a disease or an ailment that drives them to passionately act. There are endless reasons why people become passionate that are not always obvious, and it isn't always about success and wealth.

Remember, we are meeting our moment. We are staying focused on the goal to be bold and live our most extraordinary life. We want to live with the audacity to be uncommon and part of the 10 percent or even 0.1 percent . . . yes, in wealth, but also in health, love, experience, opportunity, happiness.

We want people to care about giving back to history. We want people to care about helping their community or other people as stated by Jobs. But how do you make people do that if they don't care? You can't. Just because we want people to be passionate about the greater good—something bigger than themselves—doesn't mean they're going to be. In the absence of passion, they will not have a big, positive effect on history. Unfortunately, it is more common for people not to put back into the flow of history, especially to the degree of Jobs, Gates, Buffett, and other big contributors. If all it took was to tell people to care about giving back, we'd be saved. People need to actually care. They need to be compelled. They need to have passion to do it. It's the only way it happens.

This is why you have to connect with people where they are, in their passion.

There are many successful people in business who are not necessarily passionate about what they do. There are marriages that have lasted for fifty years that may not be soul-mate, passionate connections. Passion can also make you unhappy, angry, and evil, as we've said earlier. But when passion exists and competes with something where passion does not exist, it is remembered larger, it creates a more extraordinary story, and it provokes a greater effect.

Sadly, we're a very status-quo–oriented society, so often-times passion can make you unpopular simply because you are swimming upstream. You don't have to be an evil tyrant to be hated. Vocal supporters of gay rights, Martin Luther King Jr., PETA, Rudolf Diesel, even Taylor Swift have all been the subject of hatred simply because they are passionate about things that piss people off like equality, energy alterna-tives, and even love. Some have even been assassinated.

I can't tell you how offended people get when they find out I'm vegan. You want to tick off 98 percent of the American population? Tell them you're vegan. I had an easier time coming out as gay than being vegan.

I don't believe in torturing 150 billion living beings a year so that the meat and dairy industries can make bil-lions of dollars. I don't believe we should allow world hun-ger to exist when redirecting the food resources we use for the meat and dairy industry would solve world hunger for-ever. I don't believe human beings should go without clean water supplies so we can use it for the animals on meat and dairy farms. I don't believe we should pay health-care costs that dwarf the defense budget because cancer, diabetes, and heart disease drive up the costs, when a vegan diet mitigates all three of those things and more. I don't believe our environment should be dying because methane gases from the meat and dairy industry, overfishing our oceans, hunting exotic species for sport, and wearing animals are destroying it.

I believe in compassion, and that all living beings have a right to not be tortured, and I believe that all our epidemics are connected and cannot be solved in a bubble. Human, animal, and environmental issues are all intertwined, so if you care about one, logically you should act for them all. It doesn't make a lot of sense to be an environmentalist who eats steak.

I am very passionate about this, but as I'm sure you are gathering by now, this is not the view of 98 percent of the world. If it were, the aforementioned problems wouldn't exist.

You see, even in the not-so-obvious corners of my life, I live with the same conviction that got the biggest investment on *Shark Tank*, that built an empire out of a hobby, and that loved someone so hard it almost killed me.

People love and admire my career prowess and celebrate my bold disposition. They love me for it. But when I apply that same audacity to my ethical beliefs that don't align with majority societal stances, I become less popular. They hate me. They hate that I represent a criticism of the way they are living their lives. I am viewed as a walking insult to them. It's taken personally as an attack.

I stand up against injustice and I always will. I'll never be silent about those issues, but I also believe that people want to do the right thing. I don't judge them for not doing what I do. I think that many people just don't have the information readily available to them, and I don't judge them for that, but it doesn't matter because I'm still going to be swimming upstream for representing something threatening to a familiar way of life.

And that's okay with me.

The minute I don't feel resistance or the minute I am part of the majority will be a moment of reflection because it will probably mean I fell off my path to an extraordinary life.

I love life.

And I think that's an important piece here that I have yet to mention. Because I love it, I have a strong pull to make it epic. If you are finding yourself in a place where you don't feel that way, that will require some attention early in your process.

But that's where it all starts for me.

Passion for life and wanting it to be everything it could be was the catalyst for how I turned a hobby into an empire.

Working for someone else's company, I wasn't inspired professionally anymore. I didn't feel like I was learning enough and I was just simply bored.

Alyson and I talked often about how great it would be to start our own business or invent something revolutionary. We even wanted to become money wranglers for efforts and issues we believed in, which we were already doing on the side and loved.

I loved life so much and I wanted as much of it as I could have. I wanted to own my time again. My dream was to work from home with Alyson also working from home while we built something incredible that was so much fun it didn't feel like work. I would make my own schedule, have the wealth to do anything I pleased, and have Alyson do it all with me.

While I was working at Clear Channel in Los Angeles, I wanted a lifestyle that would enable me to take off to areas of the world that needed help with issues that mattered.

My consciousness was starting to be raised to injustices that were just unimaginable to me. And like most things in my life, I wasn't going to just dip my toe into these injustices. I started consuming information like crazy about our oceans, factory farming, oil and pharmaceutical industry corruption, and anything that would fuel my now-growing need to know everything about what was killing our planet. Documentaries were a big source of that info at first.

That led me to watch *The Cove*, a documentary about an annual slaughter of dolphins in Taiji, a tiny town in Japan. The moment the credits started rolling, I jumped on my computer and looked up the main character from the documentary and tracked him down within forty-five minutes. A few months later, I got on a plane (with Alyson in tow) to Japan and traveled to this small town to speak up on behalf of the dolphins being hacked to death every year or sold into captivity. I had no idea how passionate I would get about these issues, and that was the start of this education process for me.

Once the passion was ignited, I chose to not sit quietly and let others fix it; I made the decision that I would do anything I could, and I activated immediately.

As I stood on the steps of the American Embassy in Tokyo, I was part of a five-person delegation with the very person from the documentary that won an Academy Award that year, who the world was now following . . . but I was acting . . . standing with him.

I felt that being a voice for those who didn't have one was my purpose, and it was a driving force to create a lifestyle that gave me back my time and autonomy.

Creating a Halloween attraction was like doing arts and crafts to me. Nothing about it felt like work back then. I was still working at Clear Channel, so building the Haunted Hayride was being done around my job. I would race home after work to start the night's Haunted Hayride to-do list. I'd sit at my computer until 2 or 3 AM every night, working on our website or graphic designs with our designer, who was a total night owl. I figured out quickly that emails sent during the day didn't get returned until late, so if I wanted quick turnarounds, I needed to stay up late and work his hours. It was so much fun. Often, it was pretty annoying to Alyson. She'd wake up at one and ask me when I was going to be finished, in a tone of complete aggravation. I couldn't help it; I was addicted to building this Halloween attraction.

This was it. This was "that thing" I was looking for. The thing I could do as my career that didn't feel like work. I would be so happy. Could I make the living that I wanted or was accustomed to having by creating Halloween content? I wasn't sure, but I was willing to take a loss in exchange for being so excited to wake up to work I loved every day. And if I got to do it with Alyson and spend more time on my relationship, I'd really have it all. Yup, I'm not exaggerating. The codependency brewing in my relationship was real. Clearly, that isn't exactly healthy, but it was the way it was. Remember, I go big . . . very passionate about the things I choose to have in my life.

I loved Halloween, loved horror movies and all that was involved in the genre. I could build a career in my passion of horror and have more time to be with Alyson and follow activism to any corner of the world that it took me.

I wanted it.

Once the first Los Angeles Haunted Hayride was a success, I started to really see that there was more than just a once-a-year attraction to be made here. The ideas started to snowball. The funnel of ideas going into development filled up quickly, which led to my resignation from Clear Channel just six months later.

I was now free to work on building Halloween and horror attractions and content every minute that I so chose. Aside from the personal battles I started to encounter, the excitement for what I would accomplish each day was euphoric. Nightly spontaneous brainstorming with Alyson over wine in our backyard, a new graphic that had been perfected, hitting the weekend tag sales to find unique content to bring to life the visions in my mind all made me feel guilty because none of it felt like work.

When you feel this compelled, driven, and passionate about something, it has an interesting way of snowballing or growing effortlessly. The ideas for new attractions, new partnerships and synergies, were abundant. When you love something and the enthusiasm is evident, people want to join you; they want to be around it.

Have you ever noticed the people who are the best salespeople are the ones who don't make you feel like you're being sold? You buy them and their sincerity for their belief or passion about what they are telling or selling you.

My publicist recently told me they were struggling with scheduling press around the upcoming Los Angeles and New York Haunted Hayrides. They couldn't get me moved from one city to the next quickly enough because of my obligations to the operations of both attractions.

On a few occasions, I asked them to schedule other people from my company in place of me, and they gave me a cold reception to that.

Finally, one of them said, "These bigger interviews really have to be with you. There is a very sellable quality that you have that I don't think translates when someone else is talking about your properties. You get audiences excited and enthusiastic without even trying. Your genuine love for what you are doing comes through the minute you start talking, and that's what is going to bring people through your gates."

It was such a compliment. They had been reluctant to say that earlier, because they thought I would be offended that they didn't want my team on the interviews. But I understood it perfectly.

In personal examples, passion can also be mistaken or misplaced. I have found myself in relationships that I have inaccurately described as passionate because they are highly charged, either sexually, volatilely, or both. There is little to them other than those characteristics, but somehow we put them in the "passion" bucket. But when you deconstruct them, there's actually nothing similar to passion. It's usually sickness that we often become addicted to because of an unaddressed issue from our past that is replaying itself out in our adult life. We call it passion because we are speaking from the profound feeling of the addiction.

The relationships that inspire me are the ones that are actually passionate. The people who inspire me to create, build things, want more fun, and grow and who add happiness to my world are the truly passionate relationships of my life. Being inspired is the way I want to experience passion with the person and people closest to me, but again, I had to learn that.

Without even knowing or consciously trying to find my passion, I did find it. And that is not to say I have only one. From as far back as I can remember, I don't think I stayed interested in things that weren't compelling to me. I have been living with passion my whole life. I think the danger comes when people stay in situations that don't inspire them. I found myself in that very space at Clear Channel after ten years of an amazing career but one that no longer inspired me. I was at a crossroads. I had a choice to stay or take some shots. You have the choice to stay or take some shots.

As we've said, it's not always obvious where you will find your passion "sweet spot," so in those cases, yes, it's hard to "follow your passion" if you haven't identified it. I think it's a more action-oriented exercise than that.

I believe completely that you must act with passion, you must live with passion in your value system, you must let it guide you if you want better . . . better than the 90 percent. But indeed to follow it, you must first find it. Sometimes it will find you, but often it doesn't. That leaves you one option and, lucky for you, it's one that is completely in your control. You will find compelling, meaningful, inspiring days ahead of you when you can wake up every single morning with excitement for your to-do list, with enthusiasm to see the people around you that you love, and a wish that the day would be a little longer because there is so much you can't wait to experience.

Don't settle for having this less than "every single day."

There may be the times that fall short, but to commit to this kind of living every single day will, guaranteed, give you more of those days than if you'd lowered your expectations.

Can you imagine how happy life will feel with this kind of meaning?

The best part about passion is that it is directly connected to your feelings, so when you are living happier, the people around you get happier, love and relationships work better, physical and mental health excels, success grows, and fun is more fun.

So what is there to talk about here? Don't think yourself into inaction.

Get going. Find it. Start taking those shots and take a lot of them. Ready, fire, aim.

8

COMPETITION

During my first year in Los Angeles, after I had been transferred from Clear Channel in Connecticut, I was told by my new management team that all of the executives were going to be given a Gallup assessment of our strengths.

Gallup is a highly credited, personality-testing organization that is often used by everyone from employers to the FBI to the government . . . even to help profile fugitives. Their assessments are valued as highly accurate. They are a great tool for creating a culture to manage people based on their strengths. I grew to really like these assessments and started to give them to my employees as I moved into management as well.

I took my Gallup StrengthsFinder assessment, which spit out thirty-four strengths in order of their dominance in my personality. The claim is that everyone has some degree of all thirty-four of these strengths, but the volume is turned up higher on some than others, and it's different in everyone. The top five are known as your "Signature Strengths" and the ones that, for all practical purposes, determine who you are.

My top five or Signature Strengths were (in order): Competition, Achiever, Responsibility, Futuristic, Focus. I mean, can you say heart attack waiting to happen? That is some galactically intense shit. Number six was Activator.

My dominant strength is competition. Sounds about right.

When I started Ten Thirty One Productions in 2009, there wasn't another company doing what we set out to do. We had a pretty clear lane with little competition in an apples-to-apples way. There were other Halloween attractions in the marketplace, but they weren't being produced by companies with an entire focus on the Halloween and horror industries. They were amusement parks that went to Halloween content for a few weeks, then switched back to their original content for the rest of the year.

With the exception of three major amusement parks, two of which were over forty minutes away, the Los Angeles Haunted Hayride would have very little competition. We were the newest and only independently run attraction in

LA, and the first and only haunted hayride ever in Southern California. It was incredible that a market the size of LA was so underserved for this giant six-billion-dollar (at the time) holiday.

We were able to come into the Los Angeles market for the first time with very little competition. Because of our unique model and being the first to jump into the pool of bringing city-dwelling Angelenos into the woods at night—something that is highly unusual in the concrete jungle of LA—we were an instant hit.

We were first because the moment we had the idea, we took the shot. No waiting, no overthinking . . . just shooting. We needed to get there first. And we did.

When you think of other industries, there is typically a clear leader. It's most often the one who got there first. Not always, but often. And without a doubt, when you're the first, it's yours to lose.

And I will throw that gauntlet down very clearly . . . we were first, we are leading now . . . and I want to lead even more in the coming months and years.

In 2009, there were four Halloween attractions to speak of in LA. Only one was not an amusement park: Los Angeles Haunted Hayride. During the Halloween season that finished in 2015, there were twenty-six Halloween attractions.

Call me a narcissist but we started something.

LA Haunted Hayride did something very interesting. We made it look easy. Two girls that nobody had ever heard of erected a big, beautiful Halloween attraction that pulled in tens of thousands of people from all over Southern California. There wasn't a big corporation behind it, no celebrity name to speak of, not even a little corporation that anyone had heard of . . . just two thirty-year-old girls who loved decorating the hell out of their house and throwing parties at Halloween.

"Well, if they can do it, I can do it" seemed to be an echo that would haunt me in my sleep for the upcoming years.

Competition was born.

Light would start to be cast on the dark-horse industry of Halloween attractions. It was a sexy and alluring endeavor but gave a very false sense of security to potential competitors, as it wasn't nearly as easy as it looked. As quickly as the new attractions came, they also went. Not one new attraction in Los Angeles from 2010 to 2014 came back in 2015. Attractions linked to famous names of icons in the horror world have exploded onto the scene with visions of mountains of money and books of amazing press and accolades just to fall, never to return—at best they'd move to another city.

Why? Because, it's really hard. It's not nearly as easy as its seductive call would have you believe. And these days competition is fierce . . . and a blast.

There is something so invigorating about competing and watching competition. When more Halloween attractions started popping up, it was energy. It was an energy that was starting a frenzy . . . a feeding frenzy. And the frenzy just made that world bigger because attention is contagious.

Could anything be more fun than this type of competition?

You must evolve every day; you must stay ahead of trends; and you have to hunt for treasure in unusual places and see treasure in trash. You must prevail or cease to exist. Every day you hit the ground, knowing it could be your last. The stakes are high and when you are driven by a competitive disposition, nothing can be more motivating. Not money, not relationships, not creativity . . . just winning.

You'll start to see our prior discussions about passion, activation, and choice work in the realm of competition. We'll start to look at how these themes affect competition and outcomes, and how even those of us who aren't competitive can still thrive in a competitive environment.

Competition can consume you. It can push you to achievements you never thought possible. It can cloud your judgment, make you excited or angry, and a host of other emotions. It's also a fantastic thermometer. If you have any doubt whether you're on to something or good at something, look around you to see if there's a line of people ready to compete or copy you.

I started to think about how competitive I was, in a cerebral-awareness kind of way, in my early twenties. I had just broken up with my first love and turned to cardio kickboxing as my outlet, which was just starting to become giant. It was exhilarating. There was such a sense of team in those classes. The other class members followed the instructor from venue to venue to take his classes. I realized it was something pretty special . . . not just another cardio class. The music was driving and would blast through the room while we threw a myriad of different types of punches and kicks into the air and into big punching bags. We left it all in that room, exiting with nothing but a few steps left in us to get to our cars.

The instructor, Dennis, was an actual fighter who was actively engaged in tournaments. His instructor was the owner of a kickboxing school and also a very skilled fighter and an active competitor. I was immensely intrigued by the fact that they were actual fighters. After a few short weeks, it appeared I was getting pretty good, quickly. Dennis approached me and asked me if I would ever consider competitive fighting. Well, that was it . . . you can't ask me a question like that and ever think I'm going to walk the other way. The question alone felt like I was being challenged. There was no way I wasn't going to start down that road. And once I start something, the challenges and competitiveness just keep pushing me farther.

I started training with Dennis and his instructor Les, traveling wherever they were training each day. I was going all over the state of Connecticut to learn the skills to get into a ring and compete and hopefully not get seriously injured.

It appeared I was uniquely talented at this weird new sport and also really fast. They registered me for my first fight and I was terrified. Being that terrified meant I had to do this even more. I was never going to show that I was terrified so

I just got quiet, which made me look tough—it seemed to be a good strategy.

The day came for my first competition. It was intense. I waited for what felt like an eternity for my match to be called, and when it was, I was ready. I stepped onto the mats and fought against a girl of similar dimensions, and after three long rounds, I won.

My instructors were elated. They soon started to put me in every tournament in our area and I kept winning. There was one girl who was undefeated and had kicked the living shit out of another girl from my school in a prior tournament. She was huge, strong, and had been a fighter her whole life as was the rest of her family. My instructors wanted to put me in the ring with her. She had never lost, and everyone expected me to change that. I was beyond stressed out. But of course the challenge of it, the competitiveness that drives me as the number-one strength that Gallup later told me decides who I am, could not let me lose this fight. As nervous as I was, I was not going to let this massive, undefeated chick keep her title. Looking back, I realize I wasn't nervous about fighting her or getting my ass kicked. I was nervous about not winning. I have now learned that the biggest part of my stress and anxiety comes from the fear that I will not win.

When I am negotiating a deal, I'm pressured most by victory—not the issues of the deal. I need the deal to be my way . . . I need to win. It's a great motivator and often pushes me so hard that I do indeed win. However, it can also hinder me if it doesn't allow me to focus on the issues in the interest of moving something forward that could still be worthwhile and successful. It's a balance that I have learned to pay attention to, but I'll always have to work at it.

I won the match against the undefeated fighter. And it was an incredible win because the entire arena stood up and was screaming during those last moments. I don't have the words to describe how the feeling of an arena screaming and cheering for you when you win feels to a person whose number-one signature strength is competition.

That was the beginning of my addiction to winning.

Being competitive alone will not make you win, and winning isn't always a destination. Often, it's a constant reinvention that is critically necessary to stay in the lead or even just keep you in the game.

What makes you different? What is your unique selling proposition?

The answer can take many different shapes. I've stated already that, in so many instances, the only difference between a poor person with an idea and a rich person with an idea is that the rich person activated his or her idea. In this example, the person who won the competition was unique because he or she activated. You can start to see the synergy of competition with the other key ingredients we've been discussing. Steve Jobs's relentless drive to make the world better revolutionized it. It wasn't necessarily about Jobs being competitive. Passion put him at the top of the leaderboard. And now, the ability to consistently reinvent and stay ahead of technology is keeping Apple there. You see, it's not enough to get there. You must stay there. The competition lives whether you are competitive or not. And you can compete whether you're competitive or not. As I just said, passion can win. Taking the shot can win. Being smarter can win. Being more talented can win. And, all of those things can exist in a person with or without a competitive "gene."

Who are you? Where will you win? Without taking the Gallup StrengthsFinder (though I highly recommend it), it could be a bit more tedious to evaluate yourself to answer these, but it will be enormously helpful. Spend the time to find out what drives you. Learning these strengths will help you manage yourself in the same way these assessments help employers manage their employees. It can also help you get clear about the strengths that may be turned down in volume in yourself. And in those cases, you can team up with others who are greater in those strengths and really start creating a strong and strategic foundation for competing in whatever professional environment you choose.

You cannot escape that you will have to compete, so it makes sense to set yourself up to win by competing where you know you are strong or seeing where you are weak and strategizing to make that part more powerful.

For example, if you have a high degree of "woo," which means you're motivated by meeting new people and forming strong connections with them, you will succeed by building your relationships and winning people over. Focus your efforts there. Maybe you're more of a one-on-one type of person with woo who isn't going to command a roomful of people, and the thought of that just makes you want to throw up. It would make career sense for you to team up with someone who has a strong sense of command to manage that part of the process. This could be an effective strategy in a competitive business environment in which you don't have your own competitive strength turned up to excel.

Once you have become very familiar with your best quality, you need to relentlessly own it. Mediocre success isn't going to do it for us. In order to stay not just relevant but unprecedented, you must always be evolving into new, uncharted territory. Find the treasure first. Look in places that have not been touched and be unreasonable in your desire.

And for crying out loud, enjoy it. Competition is a great thing. It implies value. If there isn't anyone interested in competing in a certain area, it's most likely because the perceived value isn't evident.

And every single potential or realized competitor, demanding customer holding unreasonably high standards, press reviewer, and genre aficionado out there only augments the challenge and unreasonably high standards to which we hold ourselves.

And that's the ultimate competition for us.

After all that, it really boils down to outdoing what we think has been our best work. Because, again, we're back to it being about extraordinary, and to me that means not stopping when you win the day. Winning the day is just the start to the real target, which is not only to lead your competitors, but to lead your own very best . . . and then top that.

And when that is your sincere intention, leading your competitors will be a side effect.

9

THE TEAM

don't look for the person with the best résumé. On the contrary, I typically like the person with no résumé. It tells
me they're always working, so why would they have an
updated résumé? I also care less about the perfect skill set
and more about the sheer drive to be the best. Those are the
people I want on my team. And because of this, it's usually
a gut instinct about the way someone responds to me or a
demeanor that just strikes me. So when I see it, I fire.

Ready, Fire, Aim isn't just a work philosophy, it's an
everything philosophy for me, so it would make sense that
it's even how I have chosen my team. I'm not digging into
every skill or strength before firing . . . the second I feel
compelled, I want them. That's why a person who had no

corporate business skills is now the COO of Ten Thirty One. She rose to the occasion. That's why a person who had no directing skills is the company creative director; his talent was giant and he rose to the occasion. I've had a tremendous amount of success Ready, Firing, and then Aiming when it comes to my team.

Creating a team that can carry out a magical vision will go down as one of the most difficult parts of building Ten Thirty One Productions. It's been an emotional roller coaster of frustration, happiness, appreciation, anger, cancerous behavior, threats, intimacy, and everything in between.

It's so easy to fall back on the notion that if you're the boss, you're the boss . . . end of story. But no way . . . I wish it were that easy.

It is absolutely not possible to build a successful business without the support of a team who can make you and your company look good. There are very few one-person shows out there. Even more solitary professions like being an author or artist will at some point need the support of an editor, agent, gallery owner, or manager. The point is to get on board with a meaningful group of people who can help push the ultimate goal forward, and to do it without an ego. Leave the "I'm the boss" mantra at the door. Better yet, throw it in the closest dumpster and never look back. That's only step one.

Though we live in a nation with 325 million human beings, the pool of talented candidates is limited at best; the pool of passionate candidates is scarce; and if you're looking for someone who is both talented and passionate, you'd better say a prayer and hope the tooth fairy leaves them under your pillow because that's about how often they just come along.

At this point, you probably feel as though you know me well enough to guess that I'm not going to be satisfied with a mediocre team of talent around me. The people I choose to represent Ten Thirty One Productions are a direct reflection of my company and of me. And secondly, these individuals need to be able to carry my vision. It's horribly sad that these types of employees have become such an endangered species.

Somehow we have wound up in what I believe to be an incredibly unemployable population. The level of entitlement from young adults just coming out of college or just entering the workforce is mind-blowing. I am speaking just of my experience from hiring, managing, and firing employees at Clear Channel Entertainment in the corporate sector, and then of course from building Ten Thirty One Productions from the ground up. The old-fashioned work ethic that has seemed to diminish over time or at least become harder to find. I've experienced all too often a really disturbing demeanor where applicants seem to think the employer needs them more than they need the employer. And they're not always wrong.

I'm incredibly lucky with what I have to offer candidates these days. I have a really sexy entertainment company that focuses on content (horror) that naturally yields a high passion level for those who consume it. And since I'm the only company doing all horror all the time, the pool of passionate candidates may feel a little more abundant to me. And to be clear, I use the term "abundant" very loosely. So they come to me passionate about horror—that's great, but what else? Well, most often, nothing. This has been the single biggest challenge I have been faced with since Ten Thirty One Productions started growing.

Today, in 2017, going into our eighth year, I have eight full-time annual employees. Three of the eight—the creative director, chief operating officer, and senior producer—have been with me since day one in 2009. These three are the dream, the candidates you hope you can uncover if you kiss enough frogs. But, sadly after eight years, I can say I have yet to see anyone else come through our doors who has the perfect storm of qualities that these three have. The other five on the team are key players for whom I have high hopes, and they could be at the level of my "perfect stormers," but only time will tell, as I have come to learn.

The TTO creative director and chief operating officer started as a husband and wife makeup-artist team. They were working in theaters and on cruise ships, and they saw an employment ad the senior producer (who was an assistant at the time) had posted for our first-ever LA Haunted Hayride. They contacted her because they were huge horror connoisseurs and had a genuine love for live entertainment. They didn't live in LA but wanted the job so badly they explained that, if hired, they'd stay on the couch of friends for the five weeks and make it work. The more I got to know them, the more I could tell they had a special commitment level. These two would show up early for morning news shoots at 3 AM and take naps in the hay wagons on short breaks, then work the event until 1 AM. They loved this work, were very talented, and had a huge horror vernacular, meaning they were highly in tuned to special effects, characters, and compelling horror genre narratives and bringing them to life.

At the time, we couldn't afford annual employees so I had to bid them farewell after the season and hope they'd find their way back to me the next year. They left LA and returned to their cruise-ship jobs. They were also taking extended theatrical residences all over the country. But, luckily for me, they loved their work with Ten Thirty One Productions so much that they built their year around coming back to LA for TTO. I was beyond impressed and quickly fell in love with their energy and contributions to the company. Clearly, by their current titles, you can see that they have done very well moving up the ranks of the company and becoming an intricate part of the machine.

The current senior producer came on board pretty much at the same time Alyson and I decided to build the company. She was one of our dear friends and was producing beautiful events all over town for a well-known restaurant group and production company. We had met her a couple years earlier when we hired her to cater an event we were building for Clear

Channel. She was incredible, didn't miss a thing, knew everyone in the industry, and could hustle like a mother. We knew we wanted her help, and by this time she had become a close friend, so we enlisted her. She ended up being the one who discovered and recruited our last integral player, our production director, who completed the roster of needed members.

We had a team.

That is not to say it's been all puppies and butterflies. As with any long-term relationships, struggles are unavoidable. And these relationships have been no different. We've hit some serious bumps along the way, some that could even be described as head-on collisions. But these are also the interactions I'm the most incredibly proud of because we worked to find resolution with each other. This is the epitome of creating leaders. You stick with your commitment to them even when it's easier to jump out of the plane and pull the rip cord. Every time we work through the struggle, we come out of it stronger. And these three have been proof of that commitment.

Other players have come and gone, and some of them were also incredible pieces of the puzzle that built us. Our turnover is very small, with most of the key employees staying from four to eight years and counting.

So what's the problem? It sounds like we have the dream team. The difficulty was that, after our first year, it was virtually impossible to build a team big enough to handle the demand on our attractions.

We were able to put butts in seats, but they weren't excellent butts. More often, they weren't even mediocre butts so, as you can guess, they weren't going to fill my seats. Here is where the rubber has met the road. This is where choices had to be made regarding which projects we could launch and which would have to be a slower roll.

For example, last year we've been approached by: four new major metropolitan markets who want us to bring Haunted Hayrides to their location; over a dozen people who have properties and want to do a Campout; two iconically famous recording artists who want us to build them a themed attraction; one of the most famous movie producers in the horror genre planning a new movie project; and the head of a major Asian entertainment company for an installation in Shanghai. Just in one year.

I have wanted to say yes to every single one of those opportunities but, obviously, with a team of eight, I'd sink the ship.

It's been an incredibly hard balance because walking away from opportunity, for me, is like nails on a chalkboard. Having Mark (Cuban) on the team has been valuable in these times because he has been critical in reeling me in and talking me off the ledge when my eyes are bigger than my stomach, so to speak. We've actually had some pretty contentious conversations because when he tells me to wait on an opportunity, I feel like the world is ending and want to jump through the phone. However, having a partner like

Mark is rare. Having such a tenured big-business resource to fall back on when I don't have the answer gives me peace of mind I hadn't had before he joined the team. And that's not to say he always has the answer, but he'll ask the right ques-tions, which can often lead me to my own answer. So, I try to remember that there are times when I may not be right and listen to his words, "Mel, don't drown in opportunity."

A new producer and two new creative assistants have recently been enlisted into the Ten Thirty One Productions ranks, and the new energy has been good for morale and for freshening up brainstorming and content creation.

I can honestly say that everyone on my annual staff feels like a Ten Thirty One Productions soul mate. My single big-gest challenge, in terms of time, has been to create a culture where they can flourish, stay engaged and motivated, and become leaders.

I've also learned that my best successes have come from people whom I've targeted because I've spotted something special, or people who have actively pursued me because we were offering their dream career. Not one single person on my team came from a want ad placed in an employment outlet. We did find my creative director and chief operating officer that way initially, but not for the big roles they have today. We'd placed an ad for a makeup artist, and I actively groomed them for growth in the company in the years fol-lowing because I recognized something special. This is an important point because I truly believe that when someone is special and has extraordinary talent, passion, and work ethic, they are typically not answering want ads because they already have a job.

People like this are uncommon, so their employers keep them. That's why I believe when you are starting or growing your team, you must conduct an active search, not a passive search. By that I mean you must pay attention to the people you cross paths with, and when you see someone who impresses you, don't just pass them by. Let them know you noticed them, and that you have an opportunity, and that you'd love to stay connected if they're ever in the market for a change. I guarantee you the person will always want to at least hear about your opportunity. At that point, you have a shot at selling them, so be compelling. Don't sell them like a used-car salesman; make them want your opportunity so badly they start to fight for it. This is not an effort to get you to beg because good talent is so hard to find, it's a chance to make a connection with someone who may just become your chief operating officer one day. If what you have to offer sounds appealing enough, most motivated and hungry candidates will start to fight for the opportunity. This is what I call an active search.

The passive search, which unfortunately is more common, means posting opportunities and waiting for the résumés to roll in. This method will flood your inbox with applications from every unemployed or unemployable person who lays eyes on the posting, whether they have your specified qualifications or not. This pool of people is more likely to be desperate for money and willing to take anything they can get. The problem is often that someone let them go or they quit. Both scenarios should lead you to an unfavorable conclusion. If someone let them go, it's reasonable to assume they were not valuable enough to keep or make the cut. And if a candidate quit and is now seeking a new job, it means they quit without having another opportunity lined up, which can often also be a red flag. There can always be an extenuating circumstance here, but generally speaking this has been my experience.

You'll most often find yourself spending much more of your time trying to fill positions when you engage in passive searching. So much of that time is wasted just drowning in pools of undesirable candidates. Like everything else we're discussing in these pages, navigate your path by actively taking shots and going after the extraordinary talent that may not always be looking for you. Look for them everywhere, and when you see that sparkle, fire. Or Ready, Fire, Aim!

The second piece of creating that killer team can be summed up by one of my favorite quotes. Author Tom Peters said: "Leaders don't create followers. They create more leaders."

Nothing gets me more excited about a new employee than watching them want more. When my employees tell me they want to be the CEO of the company one day, I swoon. That is exactly the hunger and motivation I want walking the halls of Ten Thirty One Productions. I don't want to hire an assistant who wants to keep their job as my assistant forever. I want them to want the kingdom.

Every person that I bring into Ten Thirty One is a person I have every intention of turning into a leader. The more leaders I have, the better our work becomes, and the volume of creating grows exponentially because then those leaders should ideally also be making leaders out of their team members. This is the ideal situation and the ecosystem of a really healthy company. And while it sounds easy enough, it's not. Aside from finding this leader-worthy talent as discussed earlier, egos can really get in the way. Power can really affect someone's behavior.

In the early years of Ten Thirty One Productions, I brought on an assistant once my workload was getting unbearable. It was one of the first annual positions I added to the company once we had the revenue to finance it. My intentions were to put every piece of information from my head into her head so there would be two of me, in essence. She was hungry, very good at her job, and had a lot of relevant experience, so I had really high hopes for her. She grew quickly. I gave her a lot of responsibility and a lot of autonomy.

I think it's important to understand that you don't foster growth in leadership through micromanaging and ruling tyrannically. I have found that learning curves are shorter, and stronger leadership is developed when you allow people to fall on their faces. Sometimes they need to fall hard because it's important for them and for their employers to see how they get back up and what they do differently afterward.

My assistant did very well with both. She took the responsibility and soared, and the autonomy was not misplaced because she was a self-starter and didn't need me to give her a daily checklist. We were a team, a great team. And as I stated, I don't want assistants who aspire to stay assistants. I knew she wanted more, and she earned it, and so she moved up the ranks of the company to assistant producer, then producer, until she was named general manager about four years later.

I strive to be a leader whose team will bust through walls for me and have my back without question. That means you must pay constant attention to the way you are treating and interacting with your employees. You must bust through walls for them too. Even when something isn't my responsibility, if I can help, I do. The leaders of my life did that for me, and those are some of the most pointed memories of my relationships with them.

My assistant was experiencing some personal issues that I'll keep private, but they were serious in nature, and it was clear she needed help. Because she offered so much support in my life and was such a big part of Ten Thirty One, of course I wanted to help her out, so I did and covered travel expenses and some other items. I felt like it was the right thing to do. Occurrences like this would happen every once in a while, and I was happy to help, if I could. Exceeding expectations with your actions and compassion help to build solid trust and a good partnership, which are invaluable to the team.

Sadly, as the years went on and her power started to grow, so did her ego. She started to treat the very people she had been working next to for years with disrespect and impatience, including me. The staff who worked for her during events cringed when she was in the area and didn't dare step out of line due to fear. I take responsibility for letting it get to that point. I should have noticed it happening, but I had put so much of the day-to-day management into her hands that I didn't see how destructive her leadership had become. It was actually the opposite of leadership. The whole team felt like there was a black cloud sitting on top of us each day. She spoke in short and aggressive tones, and if something didn't go her way, she'd storm out and start crying. It was bad.

In the cloud of her ego and self-righteousness, she started making colossal mistakes—mistakes that would cost the company money and make us look less than extraordinary. Finally, one error was big enough that it cost the company tens of thousands of dollars, and that was the final straw for me. Upon requesting a meeting with her the following week to discuss this and many other items, I received, in response, her resignation letter. Clearly, she saw the writing on the wall.

I cannot even begin to describe how quickly the team's energy improved. It didn't just improve—the team seemed elated.

When you're living inside a dysfunction, it's incredibly hard to see outside of it. But when you finally do step outside of it and look at it from there instead of within, it's so much clearer. You can see how bad it really feels or felt.

This gave me the clarity to never make that mistake again.

Despite the dissonant ending, I did appreciate her years of valuable service to the company and to me.

The point is to lead.

Lead ethically and morally. Treat your team fairly but not necessarily equally. Find the most impressive candidates and give them everything they need to rise to leadership. And when the team wins, give the team the credit. Hold up your best talent into the spotlight and let them feel the rewards of strong leadership. When the team loses, let them feel that too. And when you feel compelled to step in, to mop up the messes of the loss, don't. Let your prospective leaders find the solutions and the lessons. And even when someone you've supported in ways that transcend your position as an employer fails to recognize it, act with integrity and love. Because, remember, even if they're no longer in your organization, the eyes of your future leaders are still on you, and they are the circulatory system of your company.

Your staff is the most important asset you have for maintaining the health and sustainability of your company. Don't underestimate this relationship, or you will find yourself in the profession of recruiting.

10

AN EMPIRE IS BORN

The smell of coffee was making its way into my bedroom and, as excited as I get for my first cup each morning, even that wasn't getting my eyes open.

It was a really early morning for me. The team was putting in absurd twenty-hour workdays, and physical shutdown was starting to creep up on us.

This morning started even more unusually early due to a news segment covering one of our attractions.

The Great Horror Campout was on the horizon and the buzz around Los Angeles was on high. One local newscast was going to do a pretty significant piece sprawling across several segments of their morning programming. We were talking about millions of viewers throughout SoCal, because it was the most popular morning show.

As it was the third year of the Great Horror Campout and the seventh year of our life as a company, I had been around this block before. We'd been featured on every major news station in LA, not to mention those in most other large West Coast cities as well. It escaped me that morning how incredible it would be, yet again, to tell all of LA about my creation. I'm sure it was the fact that I just wasn't awake yet.

The piece looked fun and inviting. Campout came across as one of the most unique and immersive experiences an adventure seeker could be lucky enough to attend. And the team was depicted as creative geniuses. As soon as the piece started airing, calls and emails from friends, family, and prospective new customers started filling up our bandwidth. It was all falling into place just as the publicity plan had scripted.

Not a bad start to the morning.

As they wrapped up the coverage that day, I was finally waking up as my fourth cup of coffee was taking effect. I got overwhelmed by the girth of what I had created. When I looked at one news segment or one piece of publicity by itself, I missed that grandeur. I had been keeping my head down that morning, but picking it up, seeing the whole sky above me, the world in which I existed was revealed. I couldn't believe one event at a time, season by season, one hard step after another, one early morning news segment followed by another and another . . . and with each and every painstaking and beautiful year, we were becoming an empire. What started out as a singular idea to create one Halloween event in one market had turned into a multimillion-dollar, twelve-month-a-year, national-footprint, entrepreneurial fairy tale, with influencers and the brightest minds of the business world vying to jump in and help write the next chapters.

Good for me. Why should you care about my pontifications of grandeur?

I'm going to give you several reasons why you should care, and why this should motivate your empire goals, but none of them are as pointed in my opinion as this one:

I am you.

I did not come from privilege. I didn't have a little black book of magic power-player connections. I'm not a genius.

And maybe you do have privilege, a black book, or genius on your side. Great—you're starting out with more than I did.

I am just like you and I built an empire.

What I did have was a piece of information that filled a hole in the marketplace. I had a unique idea that was missing. A product that the market wanted, needed, craved, but didn't exist. It was such an obscure idea, the marketplace didn't even know it wanted, needed, or craved it . . . but I believed I knew it. And more often, you will need to know that the market craves and needs your concept even if no one else knows that. We can refer back to activating on ideation from chapter 2 to dig deeper into what to do with your idea, but this is more about evaluating your concept for its potential in building an empire.

What can you provide to the marketplace or world that it doesn't already have, and why will they want it?

I lived in one of the most populated cities in the country and, like millions of others, was a transplant from Small Town, USA. I missed the fall and Halloween activities of my hometown. For everything a big city had to offer, it had little to quench my thirst for a visceral and immersive experience of autumn. We lived in a concrete jungle, and how many movies, dinners, store displays, and pumpkin patches in parking lots can we experience and still feel experientially stimulated? There was something about taking all of my fellow concrete dwellers, plucking them out of their CrossFit sweat lodges and sidewalk photo shoots, and dropping them into the woods at night surrounded by the smell of hay, the feel of fog, and the anxiety of darkness. For years, this is exactly what I had wanted and waited for. With unyielding certainty, I believed others wanted it too. It didn't exist. It was a giant, gaping hole in this marketplace that hadn't been filled. Criteria number one of "Empire Quality" achieved.

When you have something to offer the world that hasn't yet been offered, you have the valuable opportunity to define a whole new industry, to write the rules. This can be tricky because others in your field or competitors haven't yet put a model in place, so you will have to muster up the discipline to work outside of an existing framework. It's a road that has yet to be traveled. It's a road that actually hasn't even been paved. You have to find the real estate, build the infrastructure of that road, take the first steps to walk it, drive it, trip on the imperfections, fix them, and walk it again and again. Without the structure already actualized, a great first step is to set goals. These goals can become the pillars or building blocks of your empire—the compass that keeps pulling you back on course.

Ten Thirty One Productions was built on the singular concept of creating a Haunted Hayride in the city of Los Angeles. It has evolved a lot since then, but it's important to recognize how critical it is to define your purpose clearly and concisely. From there you can construct your pillars or goals.

With that as my mission, I asked myself several questions.

Where would the very first Haunted Hayride in Los Angeles live?

How much would it cost?

How much revenue could it generate?

How would I pay for it?

How would I physically build it?

How do I get people to come to it?

These are the questions that produced the start of my formula and allowed me to have a plan of action with focus. I started the to-do list and gained direction.

Goal #1:

Location Scouting—Put boots on the ground until the perfect site is found.

Goal #2:

Research—Contact as many people with Halloween attractions around the country as possible. Visit their attractions, ask every uncomfortable question you can, and get comfortable with talking about money. Learn the revenues of the Halloween season and all associated or relevant industries and who the customers are. Know these facts better than anyone.

Goal #3:

Find Sponsors/Investors—Create a targeted list of people as potential investors who believe in you and another targeted list of corporate sponsors that would be a good fit. Pick up the phone; meet with them.

Goal #4:

Create Departments—Identify the specialty skills needed to execute the physical build. Locate people with those skills and figure out how to get them on board.

Goal #5:

Create a Marketing Strategy—Determine where in your marketplace you will reach the greatest share of your target population, and decide how you want to introduce yourself.

Now I had a framework. I was starting to build my own structure. A common nonstarter for people with ideas can be the lack of knowledge.

"I would love to build this incredible, first-of-its-kind road made of light and laser beams, but what do I know about construction, lights, or laser beams? I don't know how to do it."

I know it sounds a little sophomoric, but the simple thought "I don't know how to do it" stops people dead in their tracks and kills ideas forever. The notion that we are not all born with the knowledge to just create to our hearts' desires takes our gun and puts it right back in our holsters without a single shot ever being fired. The assumption that the privilege of creation is only granted to a small segment of people who are indeed born knowing how to do everything is misguided, and often I think it's an excuse for fear of trying . . . or laziness. Remember: Ready, Fire, Aim.

Of course, you don't know how to do something that's never been done before!

LEARN! But fire first.

Instead of "I don't know how," how about "I'll learn how." Another great option could also be to partner with people who have the skill sets you lack. Both are much better choices than stopping in your tracks and waking up another day to get to your nine-to-five where your sweat is making someone else rich.

I was speaking to a friend the other day who has wanted to open a pub for years. It's his life's dream, and when I asked why he isn't activating on something he would love so much that would give him the quality of life for which he is so desperate, he said he doesn't really understand the permit process of it or the money/financial piece. He has talked about this as long as I've known him, and all of his other friends have heard about this before I was even part of their group. It is literally heartbreaking to watch this incredible human being who works harder than he should building someone else's dream when he has all the tools to build his own. And this is an industry that already exists, so models and mistakes are already out there to get someone started.

So when it's jumping into the great abyss with an idea that hasn't even been proven as a viable industry, the pull to turn back because "you don't know how" is even stronger.

You have to be willing to dive deep into becoming the biggest expert of an empire or industry you want to create.

You will have opposition, and possibly a lot of it, because if it doesn't yet exist, many people won't be able to get their heads around it, and will try to sabotage the process. Don't ever let another person with less information than you about your dream stop that dream.

Flying in planes, driving in cars, traveling through space in rocket ships were all "weirdo ideas" once upon a time. Who cares.

I had an incredible career at Clear Channel with any future with the company I wanted, if I wanted it. The day I resigned from my giant job to be a Haunted Hayride empire builder, work colleagues, family, and friends looked at me like I had three heads—and I get it. It seemed absurd to throw it all away to try to make a living off a one-day-a-year holiday that revolved around pumpkins and Batman costumes. It had never been done, so people had no point of reference to indicate how successful it could be.

But I didn't care. Setting goals had led me to the research that brought me to the resounding belief that there was an empire to be claimed. I learned how to build it as I was building it and outworked everyone.

That's the final piece . . . outwork anyone trying to compete with you, and outwork yourself. You must not let "learning how" slow you down. The key is to learn as you do it. Often, we take that point to mean learn and then activate, but that can also be a trap because you could think yourself into inaction. There is always more to learn. You'll never stop learning, so you can't wait to know everything to fire the shot. If you wait until the timing is perfect, kiss your empire goodbye because the timing is never perfect. Learn on the job! Don't let someone else take your lunch while you're waiting to know everything and for the pieces to line up perfectly.

We all have the ability to be dream makers. My hope is not just to help you identify the building blocks and "talk at you" about my own experience. This book is also here to call you out. I want to show you that excuses are rampant and the reason so few people are left holding the majority of wealth and career satisfaction. My hope is that it pisses you off enough to aspire you to the top of the data pool. Excuses aren't hot.

The hole in the marketplace was there. The research told me Halloween was a multibillion-dollar industry so the money was there. I created my singular mission and started to learn as I built the foundation for a structure. It took time, money, sweat, anxiety, some dusting off of the knees, risk, and a lot of follow-through.

And on a morning similar to the one I spoke of at the start of this chapter, I opened my eyes and reached for my phone to check my email. Amid thirtysomething spam advertorials, team emails about the day's timelines, messages from a few friends, and other typical inbox items, something extraordinary crawled into my eyes to pry them open and push them wider than I could have imagined.

That was the day I noticed messages in my inbox from Mark Cuban; Live Nation's genius CEO, Michael Rapino; the creator of Legendary Pictures, one of the most exciting movie houses in the world; and horror mastermind, Jason Blum; and as if that wasn't enough to send me back to an unconscious state . . . the White House!

"The Obamas cordially invite you to a holiday party at the White House."

I was being inviting to a holiday party with Michelle and Barack.

Well . . . shit!

I had working relationships with all those people prior to that morning, but there was something about seeing them all in my inbox on the same day that really just made the world spin around a couple times.

It had happened. I had turned my hobby into an empire. There was and still is so much more work to do, but it was all happening. I had created the career of my dreams. I wasn't strapped to a desk or working on someone else's timeline anymore. I owned my time and loved every day.

That certainly got my little ass out of bed.

11

INFLUENCE

All leadership is influence.
—John C. Maxwell

I have the strong opinion that businesses and business leaders have a responsibility to use their influence in the marketplace properly. As you can guess by now, I'm not a fan of the status quo. Companies have an opportunity to use their footprints to challenge that status quo and move their organizations into creative spaces that can poise them as leaders to grow their influence and have a greater impact.

Influence can take many shapes, like challenging your immediate industry or organization to be more progressive, smarter, or more efficient. It can be used to push societal change or politics, and even just to make people happy.

I disagree wholeheartedly when people complain about using a business to push social or political agendas when it's not about financial gain. When it's purely motivated and not just in the interest of fiscal health. It's absurd. Fiscal health is awesome, but we also have moral obligations and the two can coexist. We are existing among daily injustices, prejudice, fear, inequality, failing education, and health care systems where fundamental rights are being considered a privilege and where special interests can buy elections and put themselves into positions to control our thinking. It is an undisputed fact. The industry with the most money subsidizes what we think is healthy, ethical, sustainable, the way we educate our kids, the way we educate doctors, the choices we make when we buy automobiles or food, and on and on.

As examples, the meat and dairy industries are two of the most well-funded businesses in America. Because they are able to buy elections to put politicians into power, they can create a mainstream curriculum that teaches us from the moment we enter the education system that, in order to have a healthy diet, we need the mythical "four basic food groups." By influencing government, they can get this information into mandatory teaching curriculums on a national level. There is no compelling science that suggests the "four basic food groups" promotes a healthy lifestyle. In contradiction, truckloads of unbiased scientific research suggest that meat and dairy eaters have higher incidences of cancer, diabetes, and heart disease. Objective health sources (as opposed to those whose research is funded by meat and dairy) now have decided that cancer patients are best put on a vegan diet when battling cancer as well as other diseases. The well-funded industries are able to pay lobbyists to live in Washington and grease the pockets of politicians to pass laws and regulations that will benefit their respective products. Teaching every kid in America that you need the four basic food groups to live a healthy lifestyle means more sales for meat and dairy. It also means those kids become adults who teach their kids the same thing. This is completely motivated by profit. There is no moral compass in play.

This is an obscene amount of misplaced influence. It's based on economics. Our planet is a biosphere that is finite, yet we prioritize our existence on a subsphere we have created to be infinite. When a subsphere grows infinitely inside a finite biosphere, resources run out and eventually the biosphere will die. You weren't taught about the four basic food groups or that "milk does a body good" to keep you healthy. You were taught those things to keep meat and dairy industries rich and getting richer. It's not cool to put human health in the back seat to economics.

Recently, North Carolina outlawed the sale of Tesla automobiles because some politicians from that state were getting a lot of money from big oil. Tesla threatened a lifestyle that would hurt big oil, so they influenced their way into banning Tesla, which makes electric vehicles that require no gas.

Influence is real and it's everything, but it's not only to be utilized by those mismanaging their power. So when people tell me to keep social and political agendas out of my business, it's absurd. Everyone should stand up for what he or she believes, because in the words of Edmund Burke: "The only thing necessary for the triumph of evil is for good men to do nothing."

But how do you stand up against groupthink? Groupthink is the majority, and often the mere thought of being the only one to stand up for an unpopular opinion will make you feel uncomfortable, so you'll change your opinion to line back up with the majority. Being the maverick can make you feel like you're the problem.

But you are the answer!

Speak up and speak confidently and don't back down. With this type of commitment, others will join your bandwagon. An individual in the minority, who is confident and steadfast, will create doubt. And doubt is the start.

Ten Thirty One Productions began in 2009, and who cared about the stances we were taking? We were small and unknown, but we still knew it was our responsibility to "give a shit." Even if nobody was listening!

Halloween was an environmental nightmare that created waste, carbon emissions, and pollution. I knew I didn't want to be a part of that. I wanted to build an empire and make a lot of money but not on the back of our planet.

That's where it started to grow. And it grew and it grew, and on our tour bus coming back from one of our Great Horror Campout cities up north, I opened my email and found this . . . "You are invited to an intimate breakfast with President Barack Obama at a home in Los Angeles to discuss issues and strategies concerning the upcoming midterm elections."

Did they have the right email address?

Let's get back to that because a lot happened in between.

In our first year, we decided to find what was called a "green coach," who would help us implement a recycling program and create our goals. We created a zero-waste goal that we hoped to achieve in five years. Each year we'd implement more waste-saving initiatives in the interest of achieving that goal. One of the biggest initiatives became our commitment to build the whole ride out of reused and repurposed materials. We wouldn't hit up Home Depot for new lumber or metals to rebuild the rides each year. We refaced things that we had, and we also created relationships with local production houses that sent all their old TV and film sets to our warehouse for repurposing. We yard saled, thrift shopped, and did a really good job producing at least eighty percent of the attractions to date on reused, recycled, and repurposed stock. We drove hybrids and electric vehicles, went plastic free at all our events, and one of the biggest and most controversial changes was turning our entire concession footprint into all plant-based cuisine. We didn't do it with a megaphone. We didn't make a big proclamation of the all-vegan concession stands, and, to be honest, most people didn't notice because the food was incredible. However, those who paid attention and did notice, of course, were the loudest and hit the social boards and reviews to lambaste us for not giving them the option to eat meat.

This was our space to use influence. We vote with our spending . . . our dollars. I didn't want my company patronizing an industry that pumps so much environmental degradation into the grid that it dwarfs that of the auto industries. It was important for us to make the connection that no one issue can exist and be tackled in a bubble. You can't fix environmental crises while supporting meat and dairy, just like you can't by supporting oil. You can't fix water-supply shortages around the planet while still patronizing meat and dairy, which is using more of the water supply than any other single industry. You can't fix world hunger without recognizing that without the meat and dairy industries displacing so much of the food resource, every hungry person in the world would be fed for the rest of their lives. It's a tough connection to make for most of us because we don't get our information this way, but when you dig into the issues that face our planet, our health, our education, our awareness, you can easily see the connectedness.

We may not have started out with much influence, but I believed we would have a lot one day, and I wanted to be on the right side of history. Our demographic is very mainstream, and I thought we could deliver positive messages in a unique and fun way. Instead of standing on a soapbox and waving our index finger, we'd try to lead by example and make it fun.

Despite some opposition, which you will always face when expressing a progressive idea or anything that compels people to feel like they are doing something wrong, we stayed the course, and I think we have introduced these ideas to a lot of people. I love the Jeff Bezos (Amazon) quote: "Leaders are obligated to respectfully challenge decisions when they disagree, even when doing so is uncomfortable or exhausting."

Even if our customers don't become steadfast environmentalists, maybe they eat one less burger that week, eat a few more veggies, try to remember their reusable water bottles or shopping bags more often. To me that's something. That's using our corporate footprint to influence in a way that I felt was educational and life enhancing.

We started attaching a nonprofit organization to our attractions each year as well. Percentages of proceeds or extra donation buttons on our ticketing pages would allow us to give financial assistance to organizations aligned with our missions. The parks foundations in the cities we operate have been a big focus for that part of our outreach. The money we are able to give them goes directly back into preserving the parks where we operate, and I believe they've implemented some great progress over the years. Again, it's using our influence to directly impact our parks but in a more simple way. That's a straight financial influence. But often the notion that you can't have influence without money keeps people and companies from participating or flexing their muscle, yet there are other strategies. We all have a muscle to flex, and anyone who says you shouldn't because business should stay out of social and political conversations is speaking out of fear of standing up or of being opposed.

Companies pay taxes, so you bet your ass we should talk about how we want those dollars spent. It's not free money that we give to politicians out of the kindness of our hearts just to make them feel powerful. We are legally compelled to give them our money, so speak your mind or someone else's mind will speak for you. And look where that has gotten us.

There is a different kind of influence that exists in business that is less obvious and I think less controversial. That is the necessity to influence others to your side of the thinking fence without forcing them. Whether you're in sales or not, you need to be able to do that. Selling isn't just about an exchange of a widget for money. As a manager or leader, you need to make sure your team will walk through walls for you because they believe in you. As a business owner, you have to convince the marketplace that it needs or wants your product. Entrepreneurs have to sell their ideas to investors, manufacturers, retailers; even doctors and lawyers are selling. A degree in medicine leads the public to believe physicians have influence over health topics, or a law degree gives attorneys influence because people believe they are legal experts.

Influence can be tricky because, often, as a leader or boss, you can feel like you are influential simply because of the fact you're the boss. But that isn't always the case. Just because someone obeys you doesn't mean they are influenced by you. Influence is powerful, and you will always need it to keep moving yourself and your career forward into exciting spaces.

I do think there is a bit of an X factor here that isn't necessarily learned. There are some people who are just so charismatic and filled with passion and belief that every word that comes out of their mouth feels like a shot of dopamine. That's not to say someone can't develop skills to be more charismatic, but charisma is definitely a part of influence that can take someone a long way. People like to align themselves with things and people that feel good.

Aside from the God-given gift of charisma, this is the marathon, not the sprint. It will take time to build rapport and trust with colleagues, subordinates, and even your customers. Take the time to understand what interests others, and align their interests with yours. When people have skin in the game, they become invested in a whole new way.

Each year when the Ten Thirty One creative team hits the table to begin narrative discussions for the upcoming year, it's incredibly collaborative. When that ride hits the ground running, I want everyone on my team to take pride in their own piece of real estate. There are times when it can be tricky, especially in a creative space, because ideas are so subjective that to like or not like something can be taken very personally. Compromise and collaboration are the keys in these instances. Talk about influencing and motivating—throwing up walls and dictating the creative space is the quickest way to produce a subpar product. Not only do compromise and collaboration feel better mentally to everyone around the table, they truly do produce a superior product because you're pulling from the corners of many minds with different points of references and experiences. More content from which to pull always yields a better product.

And on the occasions when you as the leader need to stop a hamster wheel to move something forward, adapt to communicate in a style that others understand. You can't always have conversations in your own comfortable living room; sometimes you need to have the conversation in someone else's comfortable living room or in their own style of communication. Speak in ways that appeal to them, and often you can lead them to the same idea without having to even throw down a gavel.

In a leadership role with influence, it can't be you as the leader taking credit or "props." The accolades should always go to your team. You're the team leader so a happy team that gets credit for being extraordinary will keep being happy and extraordinary—this creates the final product, which is you and your company being happy and extraordinary. That's what is important.

And now back to that intimate little breakfast with POTUS. That was the day I had been talking about earlier in the chapter when I said, "I knew one day our influence would grow." I was invited to that breakfast as one of a dozen or so people who were viewed to have influence in niche spaces. Since we were running in this "odd ball" horror, comics, sci-fi, gaming kid world and the midterm elections were right after our big season, we had some muscle we could flex. And we did. The next day we created our "Slay the Vote" initiative meant to mobilize our demographic to get out and vote. Simple and cool. While I have no idea how big or small of an impact it had on the election, I love that initiative because of what it stands for and because it's something we're now able to exercise in all elections and let it grow and get more and more powerful.

With success comes influence and with that comes responsibility. There's nothing more inspiring than using your influence to move progress and help others grow. It actually makes you grow in the process. And always remember, as Tom Peters said, "Leaders don't create followers, they create more leaders!"

What will you do with your influence?

12

EXPANSION

You've cornered the market and are profitable. Is it time to expand?

The thirst for more is insatiable in the entrepreneurial space. Let's face it, if we liked safe and easy, we wouldn't be entrepreneurs.

How does that saying go? "An entrepreneur is the crazy person who works a hundred hours a week so they don't have to work forty for someone else." Or something like that.

The feeling of a win or success is an addiction as real as any narcotic on the streets. And the danger, as with any addiction, is that it often leaves you wanting more of it. And what kind of "more" are we talking about? It's terrifyingly

easy to pull down the entire house of cards with a miscalcu-
lated expansion plan.

As you get more successful, more opportunity organ-
ically lands in your lap, and how enticing it is to scoop it
all up. And how misguided as well. The filter for most hard
decisions that come up in building a brand, business, empire,
product—take your pick of term—is to always come back to
your core. That's the laser-beam focus of your soul purpose
for existence. If an opportunity is not in line with that, walk
away. Of course, it's hard to walk away when you are so certain you could tackle something like a "mother," but you
have to. You need to become savvy at saying no, unless you
have play money or "FU" money with which to gamble. This
is one of the greatest lessons I have learned, and one that I
must convey.

Not only does "no" or passing on opportunities that don't
fit your core save you time, money, and a punch to the gut,
it also makes you more valuable. When you're not available
to everyone who wants you, you have a more exclusive or
important place in the industry.

I had just appeared on *Shark Tank* in front of millions
of people who knew I had scored a couple million bucks
and a billionaire partner. Not exactly what I'd call discreet.
It wasn't long until calls and emails started rolling in from
other businesses, entrepreneurs, filmmakers, actors, authors,
you name it. I'd like to consider myself an acutely aware person with a good bullshit meter, so I discarded most of it.

However, significant contacts were coming out of it from major movie houses, entertainment companies, plus some artists, and it was exciting. Landowners and venues from around the country would call and ask us to bring one of our attractions to their land or venue, and all I wanted was for Ten Thirty One to have an attraction near every major metropolitan area in America, so I wanted to engage in all of those conversations. Forget the fact that we were in no way equipped for that kind of expansion yet, but I still couldn't just say no, because one of the hardest parts of getting this company started was the location-scouting process. It's long, expensive, very political, and uncertain, so having a growing database of locations coming to me was a "dreamboat" life.

Simultaneously, upcoming horror film releases were proposing projects to us that entailed giant productions that supported their movies; some filmmakers wanted us to read scripts, hoping we'd let them use our sets and attractions on off nights to help with their production. We've even had two of the biggest musical stars in the world ask us to create attractions for them, which we did and which they loved, but have yet to see the light of day . . . because this work is not as easy as it looks.

My head was spinning. I wanted to do it all but was also working around the clock just to keep our successful ongoing projects on track. My focus in expansion was diluting my focus on the core, which was the gold that was already growing. And in one of the instances when I have really appreciated Mark Cuban as a sounding board, I'd briefed him on all the opportunities that we had in front of us and how I wanted to do everything but had no idea how that could happen without a bigger infrastructure, and he said, "Say no. Don't drown in opportunity!" And subsequently, he'd come to remind me of this several more times as we continued working together.

It was so simple. Often the most comforting words are. He recognized that growth doesn't happen overnight and he wasn't holding me to an unrealistic timeline. My issue was me.

I have an incredibly high expectation of myself. I'd even call myself my own worst enemy. My old boss at Clear Channel used to tell me that I was the easiest person to manage because he didn't have to manage me at all; I'm harder on myself than he could ever be. When Mark threw down two million to invest in this passion project I had created, it was like a gunshot at the beginning of a race, and I put an expectation of growth on the company that was fast and unrealistic because I wanted Mark to get a return on his investment quickly. But that isn't a smart expansion plan.

I severely restructured my strategy around our business expansion in terms of what kinds of projects I'd entertain. We wouldn't take on any responsibility that wasn't in the wheelhouse of the core of our work. I wasn't even going to take calls for proposals that didn't pass that filter because it's too easy to get stuck in the hamster wheel on calls and emails all day if you don't eliminate those that aren't viable.

The focus got right back to creating live attractions in the horror space and specifically our own brands. Those flagship brands needed the complete attention of the full Ten Thirty One executive team, as well as me, so we had to first allot our time to those. We couldn't take on anything else until they were maximized and humming.

Expansion is such a sensitive part of your growth that even when you select the right opportunities, it can still feel like you're missing the mark. It is imperative to evaluate as you execute, on a daily basis. You need to monitor the important factors, as if looking through a microscope, so when you think you're doing everything that feels right and it's still not working, you can track what's wrong.

You can take the exact same successful model that you built in Austin and do it in Houston and miss. This is when having a group of other successful builders around you as a board of directors, or just trusted colleagues, can be invaluable.

Shortly after Mark became my partner, he flew into Los Angeles and we met for lunch at his hotel. It was our first real, in-depth conversation, and we were able to feel each others' vibes and discuss a larger direction for the company. He really liked the CEO of Live Nation and felt like we could gain from a synergistic relationship. And that became the start of one of the best things Mark ever did for us. He brought Michael Rapino and Live Nation on board. There is, arguably, not a person on the planet who understands multimarket, live-event production better than Michael. And this was where I learned another incredible philosophy of expansion as it pertained to my industry, live events.

I was coming off the heels of a New York Haunted Hayride punch in the gut. I had come to some conclusions on my own about the lackluster numbers we were pulling in NYC. The attraction was gorgeous and probably one of the most beautiful and haunting hayrides we had produced to date. Those who came loved it and had a blast. The problem was, not enough people were coming. This was our big focused expansion that had taken us six years to execute.

I sat down with Michael one December day after the season had ended and I'd had time to digest all the details. He proceeded to share a philosophy about expansion that felt as though he was telling my exact specific story . . . but it wasn't mine. It was the story of one of the biggest festivals in the country and about half a dozen others.

The philosophy was that not only do you focus on your core product, but own your industry in your market until there isn't anything left to land grab and find the right synergies that can still be your core.

Here's a hypothetical example: A music festival that was making thirty million dollars in one location wanted to expand, so they brought the festival to an entirely different city using the same model. In that city, it took a twenty-six-million-dollar loss, which means as a one-city event, they were rolling in the positives to the tune of thirty million, but in the world of big-expansion fantasies, they created more work and now collectively were only four million dollars in the positive.

So the change of strategy, according to the philosophy Michael shared, could be to add a second weekend in the market that is flourishing, and when that gets maxed out, add another festival with a different genre of music, and when *that* maxes out, buy the land. I couldn't be listening to something more logical.

Of course, we all know our own business the best, so take these conversations and make them relevant to your business as you know it.

So we've explored: first, being selective to only consider growth that fits with your core, and second, maximizing the geography in which you are the strongest before moving on to another (in our case) market location.

Third, you must scale business, which means putting a system in place to give a business the capability to thrive under an increasing workload.

The ability to scale what you've created is the most common struggle that I hear from entrepreneurs young and old, tenured or new, and one with which I too struggle. As you can imagine, scaling a fifteen- to thirty-acre outdoor attraction that requires hundreds of people to build and create, and runs for a month, isn't the easiest feat in the world. Scaling is a head-scratcher for many. You can't have super-ambitious growth without scaling your business, so you need to understand the scaling process. However, every type of business accomplishes this differently, so you're basically on your own to create the plan—there is no map. We all have to be our own Christopher Columbus when finding the way to the elusive "scale" of our business.

In a general way, I've found a couple pointers that have resonated with me and I think are great jumping-off points.

The first is to create an executive team that is truly the yin and yang of the skill sets needed for the operations. The broader the base of skills you can create in the upper echelon of your organization, the better equipped the organization will be to pass down those skills to younger executives who can grow into leaders. They will then pollinate those below them and so on, and you can end up with a nicely structured group of managers who can continue to exponentially grow the grid.

The tool I've used the most is creating partnerships or collaborations with suppliers or vendors who can take on a large capacity for things like printing, building our wagons, tractors, waste management, and even with food vendors. Finding a partner you trust and with whom you can develop a strong relationship is like having a whole other division of your company, but one that you don't have to manage . . . at least as actively.

Lastly, go through every action and process that occurs in your company and standardize the hell out of them. Every single process that can be standardized needs to be. It's a hard one to peel your fingers from, and as much as we love to have a hands-on, individualized impact on as much of the machine as we can, it will limit the ultimate growth. Become comfortable with delegating, and get on board with a less hands-on approach (for the processes that can withstand it) so that the machine can be many machines. That's the prize for putting in the time to create that kind of groundwork.

It's a very complex educational curve indeed and, candidly, a conversation about expansion is a vast world of trip wires that could easily take up its own book, as could the topic of scaling. The best part about that is if you arrive at the need for that book, it means you're there. It means you had an idea. It means you activated that idea and became one of the smallest percentages in our society who built the bridge between their idea and wealth. It means you walked into fear and came out on the other side, never to let it stop you again, and that, right now, you wake up in the mornings doing exactly what you want to do. It means you had the audacity to think your most extraordinary life was possible, and you got your time back.

You built your empire!

But if you aren't there yet, and I hope the key word is "yet," what an exciting and wide-open road you have ahead of you. Hope and promise will greet you each morning as you open your eyes and know that your dreams can be realized. It wants you just as much as you want it and you can have it. I promise.

The choice is yours.

13

MOST VALUABLE LESSONS

As we bring this conversation to a close, I think it's reasonable to say that we've discussed a significant amount of content. We've examined a lot of aspects of gathering the motivation to get your dream business off the ground, and the follow-through to keep it airborne. There are some points that will resonate more acutely with some and other points with others. My entire goal for writing this book is to inspire more innovation by disabling fear and tapping into the guts of courage. I want more of us to have autonomy, wealth, and happiness.

You can do it. The fear of the heavy lifting is much heavier than the actual heavy lifting. There have been many lessons that I've learned swimming through the stormy and beautiful climate of entrepreneurialism. We've discussed a lot of them in these pages, but in an attempt to give this book life after you've finished reading it, I want to create a list of the most valuable things I have learned over the past two decades of these experiences. First, the qualifiers to make it onto the list are that they have to be lessons or words of wisdom that affected me so profoundly that I think about them daily. Second, each needs to be a piece of wisdom that is necessary to get to the extraordinary level. Without it, I don't believe the echelon of extraordinary can exist. Third, it's executable.

1. ACTIVATE!

Yup, you guessed it. One more time for me to beat this concept into every inch of your cerebral space I can access. If one single word summed up this book, this is the word. Activation is the catalyst for my whole story. I believe with a steadfast passion that activating and activating quickly is why I was able to get the head start on creating Ten Thirty One Productions to be the first-of-its-kind entertainment company. It made an industry out of a dark-horse, multibillion-dollar undefined space. And being the first one in the pool has helped get the attention of the world, and being the best we could helped us to grow into the thought leader in the space.

Chapter 2, and candidly the entire book, covers this ideal in depth, so I won't reprise all those points. But I will say: Activation is the bridge between ideas and wealth. Everyone has ideas. It's the activation of the idea that makes you special, and without it, no idea will ever be realized. Period.

Once you close this book, you should be twitching with impatience to start and *activate.*

There will be no magic without activation. Dream . . . dream exorbitantly, scream it from the mountains, but for crying out loud, climb back down from the mountain, wake yourself up, and jump. You're a magic maker and the world needs more magic makers.

2. ALWAYS MAKE A DECISION.

These four words are my bible. I have to credit an old colleague at Clear Channel for teaching me the value of making a decision. She said to me, "Carbone, come over here. Congratulations on your promotion into management. I'm going to give you the best piece of advice I ever received. Always make a decision. Even if you don't know the answer, make a decision anyway, and don't ever say you'll think about it and get back to them."

Throughout my whole career, whether it was my corporate-sector experience or my life as an entrepreneur, this has proven its value over and over. A decision is what positions a demeanor of leadership. Making a decision will present you as confident, courageous, and one who is comfortable with power. As soon as you waffle or need to think about it, you're opening the door of doubt. If you're sending an army into battle, the soldiers need to have complete faith in your decisions. A leader who needs to think about the answer and get back to you at a later date has said "I'm not confident yet so you shouldn't be either," or "I'm not an expert."

Even wrong decisions can be better than no decision. Let's qualify that quickly so I'm not responsible for someone hitting the nuclear button. I'm not referring to decisions that send us to war or destroy forests. I'm talking about decisions being made in your entrepreneurial journey to leadership. Everyone can be right or wrong, and everyone can win or lose, but you have to create belief in your leadership and that comes with decision making and being comfortable holding the decision-making power.

3. DON'T DROWN IN OPPORTUNITY. CHOOSE.

This is straight off the presses from Mark Cuban. Shortly after we appeared on *Shark Tank*, the proverbial phone lines started to light up. Everyone had an angle they wanted to pitch us or a property that would be perfect for a Campout or Hayride. Corporations would call us to build their Halloween parties or rent out our props. Movie collaboration opportunities were presenting themselves; franchise deals or cruise lines wanting to reboot Ghost Ship on steroids were all land-ing in my inbox in a normal day.

I'm an overachiever by nature, and I don't want to miss any opportunity that could yield positive growth for my company, so I tried to do it all. I started saying yes to every opportunity that seemed legitimate, and I wasn't willing to be patient and go with "slow and steady wins the race." Life became the hamster wheel. I couldn't get forward momentum because I was struggling just to keep up with the workload.

As mentioned earlier, Mark and I discussed company progress regularly, and he once advised me not to drown in opportunity. That echoed in my head like a freight train when you have a migraine. It was exactly the problem.

Trying to take all the opportunities that come your way will almost ensure that you lose. You may want take all the opportunities because you're afraid of losing, but in fact it's taking everything that makes failure happen. Choosing the ones that feel the best; putting all your focus on those few items, will yield the greatest chance for those endeavors to be successful. Spreading yourself thin will do the opposite and just distract the focus from any one thing, leaving them all to be less than your best.

A great by-product of this lesson is the power of "no." My time and my company became more valuable and pres-tigious by choosing and saying no because we became more exclusive. Not just anyone would be accepted into the womb of our focus.

4. ELIMINATE THE NOISE AROUND THOSE BALLS IN THE AIR, NOT NECESSARILY THE BALLS.

One of the biggest success blockers on planet Earth is getting caught up in the noise or minutia surrounding the important parts of our lives. Oftentimes we think we have too much on our plates and have to clean them off. A day job, kids, soccer practice, that SoulCycle class to fit in three times a week, grocery shopping—it's already too much to manage. Something has to go. Who has time to add building an empire to the mix? But which thing or things do you eliminate from your busy life? You love them or need them all.

Think of each of those items as one ball in the air, so based on the list above, there are five balls in the air. You can manage five balls. Why does it feel so overwhelming? What overwhelms us is the noise around each ball. Each ball creates sub-balls around them, or noise. The noise around the core of what you love or need is what keeps us spinning. We then become so focused on the noise that we lose focus on the actual point at hand, the core of the need.

Grocery shopping is one theme, but if you look at how many times it comes up in a week, it's undervalued as one ball. If three days a week you notice you're out of creamer, bread, olive oil, and have to make a special trip to the store for one or two items, that's noise. Getting in your car and driving ten minutes to the store is noise; waiting in line at the store is noise. You've now created six additional trips to the store, line waits, etc. . . . at least seven balls of noise have been added to the one ball in the air called "grocery shopping." If we use that formula across all the balls in the air, we have five core balls with seven noise balls stuck to them, which now means we are juggling thirty-five balls.

My proposal is to eliminate the noise around the balls, *not the balls.*

Soccer, SoulCycle . . . these are what we love. Don't eliminate the part you love. Eliminate the part you don't love. *The noise.* Eliminate that shit. Don't sacrifice the SoulCycle class, aka your health, because you just realized you need olive oil for tonight's dinner. Either use an app like Postmates for delivery or order takeout. If you don't have Postmates, use any grocery delivery service. They are out there. I was just in Nebraska and even they have grocery delivery options, so there's no excuse. There is always another way; you just have to be willing to build an infrastructure around your life that makes the minutia disappear from your head so you can focus on the primary ball, not the noise balls. And creating the infrastructure takes a commitment of time, but it's an initial commitment that, once in place, will give you your time back. That infrastructure could take you from thirty-five balls down to the five primary juggling balls, but even if it takes you down half, to seventeen or eighteen, you are still winning. Set up all your bills on automatic billpay;

the ones you can't can be set up as payees in online banking. Dedicate a board or space at home to add items needed throughout the week at stores and make one trip per week. If something falls outside of that trip, use Postmates or take out and don't budge on that rule. Create rideshare programs for practice, or split up the duties with others in your house; post a communal calendar that has SoulCycle days listed and create boundaries around that time. Give kids more chores to do; depending on your financial resources, hire an assistant to take over things like managing plumbers and car repairs, booking travel, and anything else considered a time suck of your attention away from the prize. Assistants can range from a person who manages your whole life to a part-time student at the local college needing extra work. The point is to take the time to create a model that removes the noise from your plate. Create that once, and sit back and watch your time return—those hours you reclaim can be spent building your empire.

5. DON'T THINK YOURSELF INTO INACTION.

This is our internal fear kicking in to make us believe we are justified in turning around and not going for it. We pretend it's the most rational and logical path . . . to stop or keep thinking *forever*. Someone can look like the perpetual researcher—a person who investigates forever to become an expert but never feels she or he really has all the answers, so they're happy to keep researching. It can be the person we talked about in chapter 10 who feels like they just "don't know how," so he or she never does, or a host of other excuses a person can think of to veer them away from the direction of their most extraordinary life.

This lesson is about not being afraid to call yourself out and to recognize when you're not activating because of fear, that your overthinking is there to justify the inaction. I promise that, while you think, others will activate and eat your strawberry rhubarb pie right out from under you. This is in essence the core of what this book is about. Take the shot, take a hundred shots before anyone else even has their gun out of the holster. You may miss half of them, but who cares because that means you hit half. You may miss ninety-nine but that means you hit one, and one is often all you need. The overthinker's gun is still in the holster, which means they didn't hit anything at all. And regardless of what you hit, at least you can stop overthinking and get back to living. Ready, Fire, Aim.

6. THE TIMING IS NEVER PERFECT.

If I just had a little more capital . . . Once the kids are out of school and I have more free time . . . When I reach the job title to which I've been aspiring . . . When the market stabilizes . . .

I read an article that sampled 3,200 seniors over seventy years old and asked them if they felt they achieved their life dreams and aspirations. When you took the family aspirations out of the question and left it to personal accomplishments or career, over 90 percent of them had dreams they didn't feel they'd actualized. And many of them cited similar types of reasoning, in different ways of course. More or less the majority sentiment was that the timing just didn't work out or other more pressing things got in the way.

You must not count on time to deliver a perfect little golden egg into your basket to crack, fry, and eat. You wouldn't sit and wait for the universe to deliver your next meal to fall out of the sky. You go to work and earn the money, then go to the store to buy your food, then bring it home to cook it. You make that meal come to fruition. The best life to which you aspire is the same. The timing will never be perfect. There will always be something that needs to be moved out of your way. And I know that because 90 percent of that sample group would have answered differently if life's aspirations were just teed up and ready when you were. Don't count on anything outside of yourself and your own ability to outwork everyone to destroy the obstacle that tries to derail you from your path. If you wait for the timing to be perfect, you will be waiting forever.

7. HAVE THE AUDACITY TO BE UNREASONABLE.

The worst thing you could say to me is "be reasonable." I'd love to see a history book of reasonable visionaries, inventors, and road pavers of evolution and progress. Actually, I wouldn't because it would be terrible reading.

If you are afraid to write your story without borders, without using your imagination to its most interesting corners, the story will likely not be the epic fairy tale for which you are hoping. My biggest fear for aspiring bad asses is that they have the guts to jump but will put a big air mattress called "reason" below them. You can, of course, prepare yourself for any risk with knowledge and mitigate being reckless, but trapping yourself with reason can mute the special note that moves your progress into new echelons.

It was unreasonable to think women should vote, gays could marry, air travel and electricity were possible . . . you get the idea. Einstein, Rudolph Diesel, Elon Musk, Mark Zuckerberg, Rosa Parks, Pythagoras, and Elvis were all just like you and me before an unreasonable thought turned them into a societal changer who made history.

8. LISTEN MORE THAN SPEAK.

It's not a far reach of the imagination to believe that success can breed a little narcissism. Because of this, I have found myself in a lot of rooms where speaking is a validation for one's existence in the room. People will often interrupt one another or talk over each other, but inevitably, it creates a longer meeting and more convoluted action items. It's also not the best look, in my opinion.

"Don't interrupt" is first. It's frustrating and it makes you look sophomoric and more interested in your own comments than anyone else's. Others will interrupt you and talk over each other, and just let them. Be the sponge in the room that absorbs all the information. When you do speak, be concise and make it pointed . . . no fluff just to get your voice heard before the meeting adjourns. I promise you, it will get you respected and invited back. Saying something of substance is always the hot commodity in any space. Don't use jargon. Your thoughts become valuable by listening to the subject, absorbing, and understanding. Then you can spit out nails!

9. GROWTH COMES THROUGH DISCOMFORT.

In the beginning, you have to be uncomfortable enough to keep yourself moving out of the discomfort. As hard as that is to digest, you have to stay hungry and need to keep skin in the game. The pain is what sends you searching for a way out of that pain. There is probably no one who understands how much the pain of discomfort stings more than I do, so I get how hard a pill it is to swallow, but I don't think you can get anywhere special without it. I mean this both personally and professionally as I have worked through these lessons. The hard falls I have taken with Ten Thirty One have helped me to pave stronger paths and wear better armor. The personal struggles of losing an important relationship forced me to make hard changes that led me to a new love, with whom I can now be my best self.

I know it's hard. Try to find some peace in the discomfort by having faith that it's exactly where you're supposed to be. I still struggle with this, so maybe find peace in that we're really all in it together.

10. STAY FOCUSED ON YOUR CORE.

The pull to grow is strong, and it's easy for something to take you off your original course. Nothing can throw a curveball at your new venture, business, or empire like someone who thinks they have a great idea for you or something you think up for yourself that seems fun and innovative. The filter for adding something to your pool of focus should be: Is this the core or mission of this empire? Is this what we got into this business to create? If the answer is not a resounding "yes," then you should pass.

You know how many horror movie ideas I have gotten over the past nine years? At minimum, probably one a week. We aren't a movie company, and while it sounds fun and fancy, it's just not our core. We're an entertainment company that creates, owns, and produces live attractions in the horror space. If something doesn't first fit that mission, it can't go on to the next criteria. Every business begins with a singular purpose, and it's good practice to stay true to that mission. It concentrates focus rather than spreading you too thin, and it's where you have done the most due diligence and have learned the most, so stick with it until you have dominated that space to a point where you have maxed out your return. Only then should you start focusing elsewhere.

With these ten lessons that I have carried with me, I feel like I have left you with a concise but big enough view of what has worked for me and many whom I have coached, managed, and those who have coached me. These guidelines are what I've discovered through my steps in the entrepreneurial, corporate, and personal world. I try to pay attention to my life. I probably think about the details of the steps a bit too much at times, but I have come to trust my process implicitly. I trust it even through pain and discomfort, when it would be easy to doubt, because these principals inevitably take me back to where I want to go.

The other thing I trust implicitly is that you have everything you need to write your own success story and live your dreams. The hardest part is just to start.

I wrote this book for no other reason than to inspire more innovation and hope, because I believe that too many people are missing out on something that is more accessible than they think. That's not to say it's not a lot of work, because it is, but so much of it requires only fundamental ideas that can be learned and a ton of elbow grease.

I am certain there is some magic maker reading this book right now with the idea that will make her or him the next Susan B. Anthony, Thomas Edison, Oprah Winfrey, or Steve Jobs.

Is that you?

ACKNOWLEDGMENTS

Thank you, first and foremost, to my cofounding partner and best friend, Alyson Richards, who has been through it all with me, my incredible team who has been on this ride since day one. Trisha Fox, aside from being a monster producer, you're my lifer. Melissa Meyer, you have surpassed my wild expectations and amaze me still every day, and Justin Meyer, there will never be another like you. Thank God you're mine. TTO is all of us.

My partners, Mark Cuban and Michael Rapino—your belief and support has been everything. Amy Sumner, Mike Jerrick, Nico Pajon, Tammy Kutcher, Peter Boesen, Jessica Jerrick, and Gina Derosa, for getting the motor started. Best assistant (and producer, by the time this book comes out) ever, Kelly Villarreal. Our talented special FX team and their fearless leader Kayla Ward, Christopher Brielmaier and Rogues Hollow Productions, Frances Parsons, Micah Delhauer, Steve Rousso, Melissa Monreal, JW Wiseman, John Southwell, Mark Neillsen, Cynthia Salazar, and Randy Bates.

Vicki Israel, Joe Salaices, Tom Labonge, and LA Parks Foundation for your invaluable support. I could never give you enough "thank yous."

Jason Blum, Marty Singer, Bernie Cahill, Greg Suess, Cielo Alano, Todd Eagen, Linda Goldman, Michael Jackel, Greg Ashlock, Jeff Thomas, Rob Williams, Paula Messina, Randy Stuart, Anastasia Ratia, Natalie McAdams, Bill O'Brien, Mike Rich, Brett Ruttenberg, Libby Flores, Melissa Kubrin, Stephanie Senter, Richard Bromley, Logan Clare, Steve Bing, Brian Pendleton, and Sonny Mallhi.

WME, Roar, iHeartMedia, Live Nation, Radical Investments, *Shark Tank*.

All of my family and friends who have forced themselves to endure the terror of being in the woods at night just to support me.

Universal Studios, Knotts Scary Farm, and Queen Mary, for pushing standards of greatness in their Halloween attractions.

Every cast member who played a role at a hayride, Campout, Ghost Ship, or movie night and returned the next day for more.

The 500,000 and growing attendees who have walked through our gates. It's all just because we want to scare the shit out of you.

Nicky Carbone, for being the little brother everyone loves to scare after hours.

Finally, my parents, Cathy and Ed Derench, because you have put your lives on hold for six weeks every year for a decade to help me cut my expense line. I'm baffled by how much you love me.

ABOUT THE AUTHOR

Melissa Carbone
President/CEO of Ten Thirty One Productions
After a decade-long career running the largest revenue market in the world for Clear Channel Media + Entertainment; launching the first-ever entertainment company that creates, owns, and produces live horror attractions; securing the largest deal in history on ABC's smash hit show *Shark Tank* in 2013; becoming business partners with billionaire Mark Cuban then turning that into a partnership with the world's largest entertainment company, Live

Nation; what becomes clear is that Melissa Carbone, at forty years old, is just getting started.

Ten Thirty One Productions has pioneered a new industry that is growing rapidly. In 2014, Ten Thirty One Productions was named the premiere leader in the horror attractions industry, with Los Angeles Haunted Hayride being the most popular haunted attraction in the country.

In addition to the Los Angeles Haunted Hayride, Melissa created and launched Ghost Ship, a live attraction that takes place on a ship that sets sail into the dark ocean at night, and The Great Horror Campout, a twelve-hour overnight immersive horror camping adventure that tours nationally. Over 500,000 people have gone through the gates of Ten Thirty One Productions attractions to date, and it's just the beginning as the company has started an intensive expansion plan. This expansion includes their recently launched flagship Haunted Hayride brand in New York; the birth of a brand-new asset, Great Horror Movie Night, which starts each year in February; and an aggressive plan that continues as we speak.

Melissa has been featured in *Forbes, Fortune, Entrepreneur, Inc.,* and *CSQ* magazines; appeared on *The Today Show* as an industry expert in immersive entertainment; and was coined a "market maker" by *Bloomberg News,* as well as Squawk Box, CNN, CNBC Power Lunch, and many more.

Melissa was named *CSQ* magazine's 2016 Entertainment Visionary; was a top-ten finalist for the *LA Business Journal's* prestigious "Woman of the Year" Award in 2010; and was voted as one of the "Top 7 Pitches" in the history of *Shark Tank* by the Young Entrepreneur Council. Melissa was the keynote speaker at the elite industry conference, Music Matters Live in Singapore in 2015, and, along with cofounder Alyson Richards, was the featured keynote speaker at Wal-Mart's Innovation Summit Conference in 2016 at the Wal-Mart World Headquarters in Arkansas.

Melissa is a steadfast environmentalist, animal activist, and humanitarian who believes it is all connected and must be addressed together to produce real change. She brings this passion into the professional realm of her life by integrating these values into the blueprint of Ten Thirty One Productions.

Melissa Carbone graduated from the University of Connecticut with a BA in Communication Sciences. She lives in Los Angeles, California, with her two pups, Macy and Gwen; frequents her favorite restaurant Crossroads; and loves horror films, tailgating at country music festivals, poolside canoodling with her pals, and hip hop dance classes.